Songs of Solstice

Goddess Carols

a Girl God Carol Book

Edited by Trista Hendren,
Sharon Smith
and Pat Daly

Cover Art by Kat Shaw

©2022 All Rights Reserved
ISBN: 9788293725237

All writings and art are the property of individual contributors. All rights reserved. None of the writings or artwork herein may be reproduced or utilized in any form or by any means, electronic or mechanical, including photocopying, recording or by any information storage and retrieval system, without prior written permission from the author or artist.

www.thegirlgod.com

Praise for Songs of Solstice

"The MidWinter holidays are a significant honoring of the Solstice as one of the great Hinges in the Wheel of the Seasons. This little book is full of the joy and delight of those holidays – few things are more delightful than joining our voices in song, in celebration.

Many of these tunes and indeed some of these words honor the familiar (and often familial) holidays while wrapping us gently but firmly in the world of the Goddess. Get this book. In fact, get several, and invite friends to join you for warm punch and beautiful song!" -Byron Ballard, Witch, Priestess, Author

"This book of beautiful, hopeful, earth-based Solstice carols and gorgeous illustrations is a joy. Through them we are able to feel the true meaning of Winter Solstice, with all of the hope it brings for reflowering and new growth for all." -Miriam Robbins Dexter, Author of *Whence the goddesses: A Source Book*

"This magical collection of songs, art, essays and poems fills my heart and soul with joy. Growing up, I sang so many of the songs included in this book. I loved the melodies, even while the words did not necessarily resonate with me. It is a great gift to receive these songs reimagined in praise of the Divine Mother and the sacredness of all life, and to be able to share them with my own family." -Liz Childs Kelly, Host of the Home to Her podcast and Author of *Home to Her: Walking the Transformative Path of the Sacred Feminine*

"These songs made my heart sing! For those who love holiday carols, but embrace more of an earth-based spirituality, *Songs of Solstice* provides a joyful way to reconnect with nostalgic melodies while singing lyrics that express a reverence for women, nature, Goddess and peace on earth.

Sing these songs around your Winter Solstice fire and infuse your celebration with holiday carols that center on the Sacred Feminine." -Iris Eve, singer-songwriter, poet and founder/ curator of "SHE: On The Tip of Her Tongue"

Girl God Books

Just as I am: Hymns Affirming the Divine Female
What is a Hermnal? It's the collective sigh of our ancestral Grandmothers. It's a means of drawing us closer together as Sisters. It is a compilation of songs that affirm our Sacredness, apart from Man, and assures us that we are Sovereign Beings and Creatrixes, too. And it is our Love Gift of Gratitude to Mama.

Re-Membering with Goddess: Healing the Patriarchal Perpetuation of Trauma
An anthology of women's experiences of trauma—trauma as a result of patriarchy; trauma perpetuated by patriarchy; and how through personal healing of trauma the Goddess is re-membered, re-embodied and resurrected.

Re-visioning Medusa: from Monster to Divine Wisdom
A remarkable collection of essays, poems, and art by scholars who have researched Her, artists who have envisioned Her, and women who have known Her in their personal story. All have spoken with Her and share something of their communion in this anthology.

Inanna's Ascent: Reclaiming Female Power
Inanna's Ascent examines how females can rise from the underworld and reclaim their power, sovereignly expressed through poetry, prose and visual art. All contributors are extraordinary women in their own right, who have been through some difficult life lessons—and are brave enough to share their stories.

Original Resistance: Reclaiming Lilith, Reclaiming Ourselves
Through poetry, prose, incantation, prayer and imagery, women from all walks of life invite you to join them in the revolutionary act of claiming their place—of reclaiming themselves.

On the Wings of Isis: Reclaiming the Sovereignty of Auset
For centuries, women have lived, fought and died for their equality, independence and sovereignty. Originally known as Auset, the Egyptian Goddess Isis reveals such a path. Unfurl your wings and join an array of strong women who have embodied the Goddess of Ten Thousand Names to celebrate their authentic selves.

Mentorship with Goddess: Growing Sacred Womanhood
Mentorship with Goddess is a workbook – a year-long programme – a rite of passage – especially useful for the transition into autonomous adulthood – and also for the menopause journey. The programme can be undertaken solo or as a group. The specific aim is *growing* Sacred Womanhood.

New Love: a reprogramming toolbox for undoing the knots
A powerful combination of emotional/spiritual techniques, art and inspiring words for women who wish to move away from patriarchal thought. *New Love* includes a mixture of compelling thoughts and suggestions for each day, along with a "toolbox" to help you change the parts of your life you want to heal.

How to Live Well Despite Capitalist Patriarchy
A book challenging societal assumptions to help women become stronger and break free of their chains.

The Girl God
A book for children young and old, celebrating the Divine Female by Trista Hendren. Magically illustrated by Elisabeth Slettnes with quotes from various faith traditions and feminist thinkers.

Complete list of Girl God publications: www.thegirlgod.com

**Inspired by the Memory of
Carol P. Christ
(1945-2021)**

"The Christmas carols had become subliminal messages piped into the department stores by the patriarchy, to say it is the only game in town."

-Mary Daly, *Gyn/Ecology*

Table of Contents

Solstice Carols? But I thought it was Christmas! Sharon Smith	1
Sun Lover Goddess Kat Shaw	3
About this Anthology Trista Hendren	4
The Crowning Sara Star	8
Winter Solstice as it is Told for PaGaian Ceremony Glenys Livingstone, Ph.D.	9
Tlazolteotl Hallie Iglehart Austen	16
Winter Solstice Prayer Mary Saracino	17
Silent Night Mary Saracino	18
Black Madonna and Babe Sue Ellen Parkinson	19
The Legend of Frau Perchta, Witch of Twelfth Night Kat Shaw	20
Goddess Perchta Kat Shaw	23
Berchta Rebekah Myers	24

You Are Enough   26
Sue Ellen Parkinson

The Festival of Yule   27
Kay Louise Aldred

Solstice Return to Light   32
Barbara O'Meara

Halcyon Times   33
Megha Morganfield

I Will Set You Free   34
Cheryl Braganza

O Holy Night   35
Trista Hendren and Anders Løberg

Oh Holy Dawn   37
Dale Allen

Star Catcher   38
Sue Ellen Parkinson

Winter Goddess Comes Alive In Me   39
(Sung to *The Holly & the Ivy*)
Dr Lynne Sedgmore

The Holly & the Ivy   41
Chelsea Arrington

Glorious Goddess   43
(Sung to *Ave Maria*)
Anique Duc Radiant Heart

I am a Goddess   45
Kat Shaw

From the First Oak Tree, the Acorn Did Say   46
(Sung to *The First Noel*)
Kay Louise Aldred

Máthairagus Leanabh'   47
Barbara O'Meara

The Winter Solstice Carol   48
(Sung to *The Coventry Carol*)
Sharon Smith

The Darkest Night Enfolds Us Here   49
(Sung to *O Come, O Come, Immanuel*)
Rebekah Myers

Winter Queen   50
Jassy Watson

Once in Chaos, Primordial Creation   51
(Sung to *Once in Royal David's City*)
Kay Louise Aldred

Spinning the Sun   52
Cheryl Braganza

Spiral to the Centre   53
(Sung to *Away in the Manger*)
Kay Louise Aldred

Three Graces   55
Cheryl Braganza

I Heard the Bells on Solstice Morn   56
(Sung to *I Heard The Bells On Christmas Day*)
Trista Hendren

The Blessing   58
Sue Ellen Parkinson

All Life is This, Who at the Breast   59
(Sung to *What Child is This*)
Kay Louise Aldred

Snow Angel   60
Cheryl Braganza

It Came Upon a Solstice Morn   61
(Sung to *It Came Upon a Midnight Clear*)
Carol P. Christ

It Came Upon a Midnight Clear   64
Megha Morganfield

The Pale Winter Sunlight   65
(Sung to *I Wonder as I Wander*)
Rebekah Myers

Women of the World Unite   66
Cheryl Braganza

Your Love Heals All Our Wounding   67
(Sung to *O Come All Ye Faithful*)
Dr. Lynne Sedgmore

Home   69
Barbara O'Meara

Bring A Torch And Light The Watch Fires   70
(Sung to *Bring A Torch, Jeanette, Isabella*)
Deborah A. Meyerriecks

Three Queens   71
Barbara O'Meara

We Sing in Deepest, Darkest Night   72
(Sung to *Three Kings from Persian Lands Afar*)
Kay Louise Aldred

PaGaian Joy to the World   73
Glenys Livingstone PhD

Purnima   75
Cheryl Braganza

Joy to the World   76
Alissa DeLaFuente

Voices We Have Heard on High   77
(Sung to *Angels We Have Heard on High*)
Megha Morganfield

The Crone Has Come!   78
Andrea Redmond

We Sing Her Creation Story   79
(Sung to *Gloria aka Iris –*
Angels from the Realms of Glory)
Dr Lynne Sedgmore

Oh Mother Earth Our Sacred Home   81
(Sung to *Oh Little Town of Bethlehem*)
Megha Morganfield

O Girl Child of the Great Goddess   82
(Sung to *O Little Town of Bethlehem*)
Kay Louise Aldred

Yule Girl   83
Andrea Redmond

Cosmic Silent Night for Winter Solstice   84
Connie Barlow

All is One   85
Barbara O'Meara

To Folks and Friends   86
(Sung to *God Rest Ye Merry Gentlemen*)
Megha Morganfield

Hark, The Time Has Come to Sing   87
(Sung to *Hark, The Herald Angels Sing*)
Megha Morganfield

Yule Crone   88
Andrea Redmond

Go Tell It On The Mountain   89
Trista Hendren

Trim the Halls   91
(Sung to *Deck the Halls*)
Sharon Smith

Solstice Night   93
(Sung to *Jingle Bells*)
Sharon Smith

Spirit of Dawn   95
Sue Ellen Parkinson

Arc of Stars   96
(Sung to *Boston, an American Christmas hymn*)
Claire Dorey

Goddess of Galactic Balance   98
Kat Shaw

The Twelve Days of Solstice   99
Margi Curtis

Winter Solstice Day is Here   102
(Sung to *Jolly Old Saint Nicholas*)
Sharon Smith

Bus Stop   103
Cheryl Braganza

Light We Now the Solstice Fire   104
with *We Wish You a Blessed Solstice*
(Sung to *Here We Come A-caroling* and
We Wish You a Merry Christmas)
Sharon Smith

To the Future from Auld Lang Syne   106
(Traditional tune with words by Robert Burns)
Carolyn Lee Boyd

Athena   108
Kat Shaw

Alleluia! A Goddess is Born!   109
Laura Shannon

Astraea   114
Kat Shaw

Hallelujah Chorus   115
Trista Hendren and Anders Løberg

Blessed Solstice   117
Trista Hendren

Blessed Be!   119
Andrea Redmond

List of Contributors   120

Acknowledgments   137

What's Next?!   142

Solstice Carols? But I thought it was Christmas!
Sharon Smith

"What do you mean, a 'Solstice Carol' book?" a friend asked me not long ago. "I thought they were *Christmas* carols."

I took a deep breath.

"Well, long before Christmas was a thing," I began, "there were the Solstice and Equinox celebrations and the four Sabbats..."

Oh, my Goddess...

We have forgotten so much! Or, more precisely, we have had so much taken from us by patriarchal religion. Much that was sacred has since been maligned and relegated by Christianity to the realms of "heathenism" and "devil worship." Today, in December around the world, millions of people instead celebrate Christmas, the birth of Jesus, the focal point of the Christian faith. Most of the songs sung—especially the sacred ones—focus on this "arrival of the Son of God" to a young woman named Mary, spending a night in a stable "because there was no room at the inn." People sing "Silent Night" and "The First Noel."

But dial "The Wayback Machine" to a time pre-Christian and you will find songs of thanksgiving and praise, not to the "Son of God" but to the "Sun God," and for the "Season of Rest" when Nature covers the world (at least the Northern Hemisphere) in a blanket of white, and life slumbers in the long night: *the Winter Solstice*.

Pagans still celebrate this sacred season, the turning of the Wheel of Time from Summer's heat and light to Winter's cold and darkness; and many refer to it still as "Yule," from the Old Frisian word *jole* or *jule*, which, roughly translated, means *circle*. As most Indigenous People did (and still do), the ancient European people—like the Frisians, who inhabited the seacoast and islands of what are now The Netherlands and Germany, and the Nordic and Celtic peoples—honored the cycles of Nature, with its changing seasons. So, Yule and its many traditions existed long, *long* before Christmas.

Winter Solstice was a time of thanksgiving for the return of the sun and its life-generating warmth. As the longest night of the year, it heralded the coming of more daylight and shorter nights, as the sun returned in its full strength, bringing with it springtime and the awakening of life once again.

So, why a Solstice Carol book? Better to ask, why not?

Not everyone is Christian. Many of us, who prefer a Nature-centered, Goddess-based spirituality, rooted in our own EIK[1] (European Indigenous Knowledge), have found deep meaning in the Solstice, Equinox and Sabbat celebrations (Imbolc, Beltane, Lughnasadh, and Samhain), and enjoy singing songs that are based upon these sacred days/times of the year.

We, at Girl God Books, decided to create this special songbook with re-imagined Christmas carols and songs (only those in the public domain were used) to honor the original intent of late December, the Longest Night of the Year, known as the Winter Solstice.

So, decorate that evergreen, set the Yule log ablaze, put on the Wassail, light the candles, and lift your voices in celebration...

And a Happy and Blessed Winter Solstice to One and All!

---

[1] EIK (European Indigenous Knowledge), from *Ancient Spirit Rising: Reclaiming Your Roots & Restoring Earth Community*, by Pegi Eyers © second printing 2016.

Sun Lover Goddess
Kat Shaw

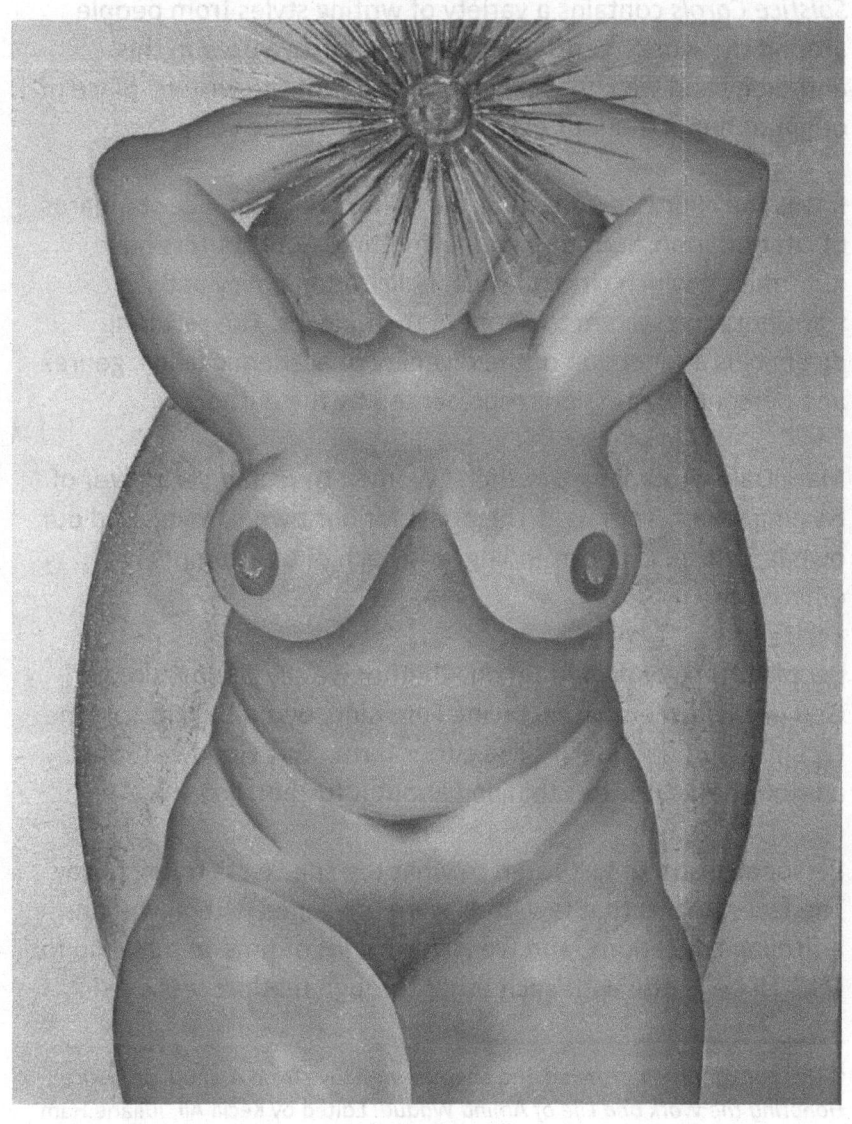

About this Anthology

Trista Hendren

Solstice Carols contains a variety of writing styles from people around the world. Various forms of English are used in this anthology and we chose to keep spellings of the writers' place of origin to honor/honour each individual's unique voice.

It was the expressed intent of the editors to not police standards of citation, transliteration and formatting. Contributors have determined which citation style, italicization policy and transliteration system to adopt in their pieces. The resulting diversity is a reflection of the diversity of academic fields, genres and personal expressions represented by the authors.[2]

Mary Daly wrote long ago that, "Women have had the power of naming stolen from us."[3] The quest for our own naming, and our own language, is never-ending, and each of us attempts it differently.

People often get caught up on whether we say Goddess or Girl God or Divine Female vs. Divine Feminine. Byron Ballard told me recently that she doesn't like either term. "Say Goddess!" She admonished us![4] After thinking about it further, I concur.

Personally, I try to just listen to what the speaker is trying to say. The fact remains that few of us were privileged with a woman-affirming education—and we all have a lot of time to make up for. Let's all be gentle with each other through that process.

---

[2] This paragraph is borrowed and adapted with love from *A Jihad for Justice: Honoring the Work and Life of Amina Wadud*. Edited by Kecia Ali, Juliane Hammer and Laury Silvers.

[3] Daly, Mary. *Gyn/Ecology: The Metaethics of Radical Feminism*. Beacon Press, 1990.

[4] Ballard, H Byron. "The Crone Initiation." Instagram Live @girlgodbooks. October 7th, 2022.

If you find that a particular re-write doesn't sit well with you, please feel free to use the Al-Anon suggestion: "Take what you like, leave the rest!" Feel free to adjust the lyrics and make them your own.

We have also included some bonus material and writings at the beginning of the book—including an excerpt by Glenys Livingstone, Ph.D. about the significance of Solstice. Kat Shaw shares her moving story about the cover art which depicts The Legend of Frau Perchta, Witch of Twelfth Night. Mary Saracino and Rebekah Myers also share Solstice Poetry, which you can read or share at your Solstice Rituals and events. Laura Shannon wrote an essay about the Goddess origins of the word Hallelujah, which we have included before the Hallelujah Chorus. As with all Girl God anthologies, we have scattered the pages with gorgeous, Goddess-affirming art!

I must admit, I have a bit of an allergy to Christianity. Male-God language grates on my nerves. That said, my dear Sister and fellow contributor, Rebekah Myers reminded me, "These carols hold appeal for non-Christian and Christian alike, as they connect us all to the cycles of the land itself, and an ancient heritage we all share."

This season has always been particularly meaningful to me. And yet, it is also a time of heightened stress for many of us. As Brigit Anna McNeill shared on Facebook:

> "The winter solstice time is no longer celebrated as it once was, with the understanding that this is a period of descent and rest, of going within our homes, within ourselves and taking in all that we have been through, all that has passed in this full year which is coming to a close... like nature and the animal kingdom around us, this time of hibernation is so necessary for our tired limbs, our burdened minds.

Our modern culture teaches avoidance at a max at this time; alcohol, lights, shopping, overworking, over spending, comfort food and consumerism.

And yet the natural tug to go inwards as nearly all creatures are doing is strong and the weather so bitter that people are left feeling that winter is hard, because for those of us without burning fires and big festive families, it can be lonely and isolating. Whereas in actual fact, winter is kind, she points us in her quiet soft way towards our inner self, towards this annual time of peace and reflection."[5]

We have included an excerpt from Kay Louise Aldred's amazing *Mentorship with Goddess* workbook to help you do just that!

I would like to recognize the early pioneers in re-writing Christmas Carols who inspired me to compile this anthology. Shekhinah Mountainwater, Carol P. Christ, Anique Radiant Heart, and Glenys Livingstone had re-writes that were particularly meaningful to me. You can find the carols by Carol, Anique and Glenys in this book. Mountainwater's re-write of *O Holy Night* inspired me to re-imagine my favorite carol. It turned out Dale Allen had written one as well—and I loved it so much that we included it too. We received duplicate submissions of a few carols, but they were completely different—and meaningful in unique ways. We hope you will find and create your own favorites.

Songs of Solstice is dedicated to the memory of Carol P. Christ. As Carol noted in *Laughter of Aphrodite*, "When singing to the Father and Son, a girl must hear her exclusion. She must begin to recognize that the power and the glory are not to be hers."[6] Singing with other sisters on Pilgrimage in Crete gave me my first glimpse of what intoning woman-affirming songs could do for my

---

[5] Brigit Anna McNeill Facebook Page, November 25, 2018.
[6] Christ, Carol P. *Laughter of Aphrodite: Reflections on a Journey to the Goddess*. HarperCollins; Reprint edition, 1988.

soul. I am so grateful that I was able to bring my (then) 12-year-old daughter to experience that with me much earlier in life. It has always been my hope that Helani will not have to spend so many decades reprogramming herself. The work of Carol P. Christ—and others—paved new neural pathways for women of all generations.

We hope this Song Book will do the same.

As we were finishing this book, I became aware of the CD by Megha Morganfield entitled *Winter Solstice Carols*. We have included 6 of her carols in this book, including one original Solstice song. You can purchase her CD if you would like to hear more! (It's wonderful!) Megha also wrote a bit about her experience of re-writing carols in her bio, which you can find at the back of the book. We have placed the quote by Mary Daly that inspired her at the front of the book as well.

We plan to do yearly Zoom Sing-Along in December—and hope to put out a CD for Solstice 2023. A second song book is planned a few years out, as many of the copyrights seem to expire then. We hope you will sing these songs in your local communities—and we offer bulk discounts for choirs.

Re-writing and singing these carols has been deeply healing for me. Love, healing, and blessings to everyone who sings these carols.

The Crowning
Sara Star

Winter Solstice as it is Told for PaGaian Ceremony
Glenys Livingstone, Ph.D.

Tonight, we celebrate the "longest night" of the year: that is, the time of our annual orbit around Sun when the dark part of the day is longest. Traditionally it has been celebrated by the ancients – our Gaian ancestors in many regions – as the birth of light, the birth of form. The stories of many cultures tell of the Great Mother giving birth to the Divine Child at this time of year. It is this Seasonal Moment for which the ancient pre-Celtic indigenous Europeans apparently built Newgrange (Bru-na-Boinne), completing the major structures there between 3200 and 3700 BCE.[7] Newgrange has been thought to be a tomb, and some still refer to it as such. But more recent research, primarily initiated by Martin Brennan late last century and documented in his book *Stones of Time* reveals something else – a large scale solar-construct. Brennan feels that the great stone bowls found there were not for remains of the dead, "but in fact contained water to act as reflective surfaces designed to interact with the sunbeam" that enters the chamber.[8] This is a very recent re-membering and conjecture about what was central to the spirituality of these ancient forebears.

The inner chamber wall of this mound is carved with the Triple Spiral motif, and at the Winter Solstice it is illuminated for seventeen minutes by the rising sun. This was confirmed by modern academia only in 1969 with minds that at that time had little comprehension of what its significance may be.[9] Some have said recently that the illumination immortalizes "earth's power to give new life to the sun,"[10] some say it is the other way around.[11] Few accounts really understand the significance of the triple spiral

---

[7] Martin Brennan, The Stones of Time.
[8] Paul Devereaux, *Earth Memory*, p.124.
[9] Paul Devereaux, *Earth Memory*, p.120.
[10] Elinor Gadon, *The Once and Future Goddess*, p.346.
[11] Anne Baring and Jules Cashford, *The Myth of the Goddess*, p.98.

at this stage, though Michael Dames in 2000 referred to the association of it with the Triple Goddess.[12] Most mythographers at this point in time have not been prepared to allow the Goddess any cosmic function, as Claire French noted in 2001,[13] or take seriously Her aspects. Another example of this is the lack of comprehension of the significance of Silbury Hill at Avebury, for so long, until Michael Dames came along with a goddess-oriented mind with which to be able to take it in.[14] It seems that Newgrange/Bru-na-Boinne, which marks the Winter Solstice particularly, celebrates the significance of Earth-Sun relationship in some way that we can only begin to guess at and re-member for ourselves. It apparently does celebrate the triple-aspect Cosmic Dynamic – as it is carved on the illuminated inner chamber wall.[15]

So, we will participate with these ancient forebears in their celebration of the Triple Spiral tonight – deepening into our understanding of it: we will dance it – I am sure the old ones would be pleased ... it's been a long time. The dance has three layers of equal significance, and it may be perceived as the Triple Spiral Dynamic, or a breath. I have named the dance as the "Cosmogenesis Dance", having learned it originally from Jean Houston as the "Stillpoint Dance". Winter Solstice is a celebration of Cosmogenesis – the ongoing Birth of All, enabled and characterised by a Creative Triplicity. It seems the ancients understood that from their rock inscription – they left us a story, a code. The annual return of the light at this Seasonal Moment is a microcosm of the birth of it All – and the Dynamic that births it all. Nothing is excluded from this triple-faced Dynamic – not Earth, nor Sun, nor you or me: everything is subject to it ... to the waxing, peaking and waning dynamic, an eternal re-creation. It is

---

[12] Michael Dames, *Ireland: a Sacred Journey*, p.192-193. He says that the triple spiral engraving "may represent the triple goddess – Eiru-Fodla-Banba. Eiru was the whole island, Fodla its divisions, Banba its hidden parts."
[13] Claire French, *The Celtic Goddess*, p.22.
[14] Michael Dames, *The Silbury Treasure*.
[15] See also http://gofree.indigo.ie/~thall/newgrange.html

the "triskele" of energy, "the innate triplicity of the Cosmos ... that runs through every part of the Universe."[16] The Triple Goddess metaphor may celebrate and express this innate cosmic triplicity.

The Cosmogenesis Dance has three layers, representing the three aspects/qualities of Goddess, the triple Spiral Dynamic that the ancients were aware of – the dynamic that they apparently understood as unfolding the Cosmos. The three aspects celebrate Young One – the ever new differentiated being, Mother – the deeply related interwoven web, and Crone – the eternal creative return to All-That-Is. The three layers of the dance may be understood to embody these. The Dance represents the flow and balance of these three – a balance and flow of Self, Other and All-That-Is.[17] It may be experienced like a breath, that we breathe together – as we do co-create the Cosmos. That is part of our job this evening.

Winter Solstice is a Birthing Place, the Gateway from the dark part of the year to the light part. It thus particularly celebrates the Mother aspect of the Triple Goddess. At this Seasonal Moment, darkness reaches its peak, its fertile fullness, and breaks into form. The face of Goddess moves from Crone quality of the dark part of the cycle through Mother at this Winter Gateway, to Young One – the birth of form, of life. This is how it happens: out of her fertile Dark Matter. Winter Solstice is a time of receiving the gift of the dark, which is birth, of form – in its depth and breadth. To help you get a feel for this, the breath meditation tonight will be a contemplation of some of the many birthings in our own lives – how we have been Creator and Created, and we will recall Earth-Gaia's and Universe-Gaia's many birthings happening in every moment and throughout the eons.[18]

---

[16] Caitlin Matthews, *The Celtic Spirit*, p.366.
[17] For Cosmogenesis Dance instructions see Glenys Livingstone, *PaGaian Cosmology*, p.311: https://pagaian.org/book/appendix-i/
[18] See the offered Winter Solstice ceremonial script, Glenys Livingstone, *PaGaian Cosmology*, p. 195-196: https://pagaian.org/book/chapter-7/

In this tradition since pre-Celtic times, and in many other cultural traditions, Winter Solstice has been celebrated as the birth of the God, and in Christian tradition as the birth of the Saviour. But there are deeper ways of understanding what is being born: that is, who or what the "saviour" is. In the Gospel of Thomas – which was not selected for biblical canon – it says: "If you bring forth what is within you, what you bring forth will save you."[19] This then may be the Divine Child – the "Saviour" – the new Being forming in the Cosmogonic Womb, who will be born. We celebrate the birth of the new Being, which/who is always beyond us, beyond our knowing ... yet is within us, burgeoning within us – and within Gaia. What will save us is already present within – forming within us. And we are *in-formed* by that which we *form* ... Created and Creator – simultaneously, in a reciprocal way. We may imagine the in-utero foetus – an image we might have these days from a sonar-scan during pregnancy. We may imagine ourselves in this way – this is a truth about Being ... we are this, and it is within us, within this moment. Every moment is pregnant with the new. It will be birthed when darkness is full. Part of it is having the eyes to see the "new bone forming in flesh", scraping our eyes "clear of learned cataracts",[20] seeing with fresh eyes.

Birthing is not often an easy process – for the birthgiver nor for the birthed one: It is a shamanic act requiring strength of bodymind, attention and focus of the mother, and courage to be of the new young one. Birthgiving is the original place of "heroics" ... many cultures of the world have never forgotten that: Perhaps therefore better termed as "heraics". Patriarchal adaptations of the story of this Seasonal Moment usually miss the Creative Act of birthgiving completely – pre-occupied as they often are with the "virgin" nature of the Mother being interpreted as an "intact hymen", and the focus being the Child as "saviour": Even the Mother gazes at the Child in Christian icons, while in more ancient images Her eyes are direct and expressive of Her integrity as Creator. In Earth-based religious practice, the ubiquitous icon of

---

[19] Elaine Pagels, *Beyond Belief: The Secret Gospel of Thomas*.
[20] From the poem Refractions" by Cynthia Cook in *WomanSpirit* 1980.

Mother and Child – Creator and Created – expresses something essential about the Universe itself ... the "motherhood" we are all born within. It expresses the essential Communion experience that this Cosmos is, the innate and holy Care that it takes, and the reciprocal nature of it.

When we light the ceremonial fire cauldron tonight, we will recall our Great Origin which has never ceased to pour forth and unfold. We receive it in every moment and in all that we have inherited from the beings and ancestors of the past, and in the infinite web we are part of in the present. It is the Ever-Present Origin, present within and everywhere – there is no point in the Universe that is separate from it. With the lighting of the fire, we will recall the Grandmother supernova that birthed our Solar system some 4.6 billion years ago – that is our lineage. We are celebrating this Cosmic lineage.

Our birthing supernova has been named Tiamat by Thomas Berry,[21] and I have adopted that. Tiamat is the ancient Babylonian name for the Great Mother of us all: Her name meaning "female sea".[22] We are the star-stuff of supernova Tiamat. Tiamat as the Babylonians storied her, was a sea-serpent in form ... a "dragon-woman".[23] We might just as well name our supernova "Rainbow Serpent", which is a name for the Creator of All in Australian Indigenous tradition.

The important thing is that we remember where we come from – our Gaian lineage – and receive Her gift. Then we may choose to express joy and gratitude. There may be both pain and joy in birthing – coming into form. The dark is not necessarily felt as negative, the light not necessarily felt as positive: Birthing may be felt as a separation, a leaving. But the new being IS birthed.

---

[21] Brian Swimme and Thomas Berry, *The Universe Story*.

[22] Thanks to Miriam Robbins Dexter for this summary of Her name.

[23] As Adele Getty names Tiamat in Goddess, p. 32.
Getty, Adele. Goddess: Mother of Living Nature. London: Thames and Hudson, 1990.

Winter Solstice ceremony is actually then, our Birth-day celebrations, a Birthday we all share. We celebrate that we are each 13.7 billion years old together with Earth and Sun. Winter Solstice is a special annual moment for expressing what new being is coming forth in you in the year ahead, rejoicing in all the new being coming forth in every moment, and the Unimaginable More that we, and Gaia will yet become.

Excerpt from "Appendix F: Teachings for the Sabbat Rituals." *PaGaian Cosmology: Re-inventing Earth-based Goddess Religion*. NE: iUniverse, 2005. (Note from Trista: EVERYONE needs to have this book on hand!)

REFERENCES:

Baring, Anne, and Cashford, Jules. *The Myth of the Goddess: Evolution of an Image*. Penguin Group, 1993.

Brennan, Martin. *The Stones of Time: Calendars, Sundials, and Stone Chambers of Ancient Ireland*. Rochester Vermont, Inner Traditions, 1994.

Dames, Michael. *Ireland: a Sacred Journey*. Element Books, 2000.

Dames, Michael. *The Silbury Treasure: The Great Goddess Rediscovered*. London: Thames and Hudson, 1976.

Devereux, Paul. *Earth Memory: The Holistic Earth Mysteries Approach to Decoding Ancient Sacred Sites*. London: Quantum, 1991.

French, Claire. *The Celtic Goddess: Great Queen or Demon Witch*. Edinburgh: Floris Books, 2001.

Gadon, Elinor W. *The Once and Future Goddess*. Northamptonshire: Aquarian, 1990.

Livingstone, Glenys. *PaGaian Cosmology: Re-inventing Earth-based Goddess Religion*. NE: iUniverse, 2005.

Matthews, Caitlin. *The Celtic Spirit*. London: Hodder and Stoughton, 2000.

Monaghan, Patricia. *O Mother Sun! A New View of the Cosmic Feminine*. Freedom CA: Crossing Press, 1994.

Pagels, Elaine. *Beyond Belief: the Secret Gospel of Thomas*. NY: Random House, 2003.

Swimme, Brian and Berry, Thomas. *The Universe Story: From the Primordial Flaring Forth to the Ecozoic Era*. New York: HarperCollins, 1992.

Tlazolteotl
Hallie Iglehart Austen

Tlazolteotl, Aztec, 15th c. CE
From Hallie Iglehart Austen's *The Heart of the Goddess: Art, Myth and Meditations of the World's Sacred Feminine.* https://heartgoddess.net

Winter Solstice Prayer

Mary Saracino

Deep night, Dark night
Night of the longest sigh
Soulful night, Sacred night
Night of the longest dreams
Cold night, Holy night
Night of unfurling desires
Womb of the world, Birther of hope
Bringer of peace and good will
Pray, pray for all good things
That suffering for all will end
That life will thrive and generosity reign
In the hearts of all humankind
That joy will rise and children will fly
On wings of prosperity
Oh hear our plea, this silent night
When the moon is round in the sky
When hopes are high and eyes are wide
with delight and audacity
May Love prevail tonight, and always
Leading us back to our Source
May we dance with the dark, without hesitation or fear
And savor her promise of plenty
Deep night
Dark night
Night of the longest sigh
May our weary hearts stay vigilant and receptive
To all that is loving and dear

Originally published in *Celebrating Seasons of the Goddess*, Edited by Dr. Helen Hye-Sook Hwang and Dr. Mary Ann Beavis. Mago Books, 2017.

Silent Night

Mary Saracino

'Tis the season of deep silence
Of dying leaves
And waning light
Of death, or what seems like death to unseeing eyes
Of long nights and even longer longings
Of quiet dreams and restless hopes
Of sitting silently by the fire, resting our cold bones
As the Earth offers her stark beauty as a gift

Originally published in *Celebrating Seasons of the Goddess*, Edited by Dr. Helen Hye-Sook Hwang and Dr. Mary Ann Beavis. Mago Books, 2017.

Black Madonna and Babe
Sue Ellen Parkinson

The Legend of Frau Perchta, Witch of Twelfth Night
Kat Shaw

You have probably never heard of Her – I certainly hadn't until my daughter sent me this information. But if you happened to be living in Bavaria or Austria during the Middle Ages, you might have been quite troubled by her during the Yule period! This was the time that Frau Perchta would be on the loose, doling out punishments and rewards for the naughty and nice.

The "official end" of Yuletide in many traditions is January 6th, also known as Twelfth Night or Feast of the Epiphany. It was on this night that Frau Perchta would drop in for a visit. If you had been good over the past year, you would be rewarded with a piece of silver. But if you had been bad – watch out! Frau Perchta was a stern distributor of justice. In fact, she was also called "the belly slitter" because her apparent punishment for bad behaviour consisted of Frau Perchta cutting open the offender's stomach, removing the inner organs, and replacing them with straw and pebbles.

But, Perchta has a very interesting story. She wasn't always an evil witch. In fact, she was at one time a greatly loved Germanic goddess, also called Berchta or Bertha, which literally means "bright" or "shining one". In ancient, pre-Christian times, Berchta was a powerful figure, worshiped by both Celtic and Germanic tribes. It was her job to protect babies, women and children. She was associated with birch trees, was a protector of forests and wildlife, and was associated with the cycle of life, death and rebirth. She was depicted as a beautiful woman with long hair, often called the White Woman or the Lady in White. She was considered a triple goddess (perhaps because of her association with life's cycles) and was able to take on forms of the maiden, mother and crone.

Berchta also had shapeshifting abilities. She was described as sometimes having the feet of a goose, and she also took on the form of a swan. As the protector of animals, she was called "Guardian of Beasts".

In the later, scary tales of Perchta, she is represented exclusively as a crone – more specifically, a scary old hag with a face made of iron and a nose like a beak, carrying a knife beneath her cloak (in case she needs to slice open someone's belly!)

So how did Berchta become Perchta? How did this benevolent goddess get demonized and transformed into an evil witch? Three words: The Medieval Church.

Christianity became powerful in Bavaria in around the 6th century. The Pagan cults that had evolved around Berchta were pretty strong and set in their ways. Worshippers of Berchta refused to be absorbed into the new Christian traditions. And so, for conversion purposes, the Church resorted to fear.

Her name was changed, among other things. The word "perchten" means scary monsters, so Berchta became "Perchta, leader of the Perchten." Berchta, the wise white lady, was thereafter known as Perchta, a crooked-nosed, belly-stabbing hag. There were tales of Frau Perchta capturing children and eating them. There were tales of Frau Perchta as the Christmas hag, who would stuff the bad kids into her giant sack. She would visit on Twelfth Night expecting food as an offering, but if she was displeased with what someone left, she would slit the person's belly open. She was also a stickler for clean homes, and the completion of spinning. So, if women had neglected their housework, they could expect the belly slitting as well.

The repression of Berchta and subsequent scary tales of Perchta took place during an interesting period. In Europe, the years between 1450 and 1700 are known as The Burning Times. During these years, Protestant Reformations began, splitting the Christian

Church into various factions. Instability caused even more paranoia. It is estimated that around 100,000 men and women were put to death for witchcraft, many of them burned at the stake.

Germany, a major proponent of the Reformations, was one of the worst offenders. Historians report that entire populations of women in towns and villages were sometimes eliminated.

Despite the church's attempts to get rid of Berchta, my daughter has chosen to keep her alive, which is why this painting is named after her. The goddess Berchta will never be forgotten. Her bright beauty is evident in Yule's return of the sun, in the new fallen snow, in white swans and in the magnificence of the Alpine Mountains she hails from.

Note from the editors: Thank you Kat Shaw for sharing your incredible artwork with us—and to your daughter Maya Shaw for researching the backstory that you so eloquently shared here!

Goddess Perchta
Kat Shaw

Berchta
Rebekah Myers

Berchta, goddess of the slender birch,
Lady, young and old, free from all blame,
She whom jealous men renamed, "Perchta,"
and demonized, diminished and defamed
into a hungry belly-slitting hag —
Upon this twelfth night you will rise again.

Your younger sister, Holle,
Dwells mid-land
and shakes her feather bed
to bring the snow.
She shares with you those aspects
known to each —
spinning wheels, and wells, and winter's flow.

Your watch is in
the southern Alpine clime,
and there you guide
the children gone too soon,
with gleaming threads
thrown from your spindle bright;
with warp and woof
cast from your shining loom.

Mother's grieving hearts
you comfort well.
With visions and with whispers
you assure,
that their loved babes
are shielded from harm;
held safe within
your tender power and care.

Women, you protect and oversee
in household tasks,
in spinning and in lore,
reproving those who
sometimes lax may be,
rewarding diligence and industry.

Shapeshifter,
with one foot of a bird,
you walk, attended by
both goose and swan.
Through the pale birch wood
oftentimes you glide,
wearing a cape of
softest feathered down.

And further on
down through the years of time,
the children's stories you will keep and tell
with rhyming wisdom
to delight their hearts —
the Mother Goose,
of whom we know so well.

And in the wild procession of the gods
across midwinter's darkest midnight sky,
you ride, a psychopomp, to all lost souls
who with you, in the wild hunt fly by.
On this twelfth night of our Yuletide
on this night of illumed epiphany,
we think of you, as one, remembering
Bright Berchta — and your true identity.

Copyright © by Rebekah Myers, 1/6/22

You Are Enough
Sue Ellen Parkinson

The Festival of Yule

Kay Louise Aldred

Welcome to December. The Earth is quiet, introverted, and internal. Roots are receiving nutrients, strengthening, and preparing. Stabilising is the priority. Externally, there are preparatory signs of the return of the Light as buds are visible. It is cold and dark, and the energy is hardly moving. The Earth is deeply hibernating and in conservation mode. There is a deep period of calm and stillness during the time of this festival. This is a liminal space for even deeper internal journeying and receptivity, gaining insight from the lower and upper worlds.

The festival of Yule, the Winter Solstice, occurs when the wheel of the year pauses again, halfway between Samhain and Imbolc. The calendared dates for the festival are December 20th to 23rd. On this mid-winter's eve, darkness is dominant as we experience the longest night and shortest day. Every part of nature is silent, motionless, suspended. We feel, along with Gaia, cocooned in the womb, preparing for the journey down the miracle and bliss of the red rich velvety menstrual bleed and the birth canal and the manifestation of our visions and dreams. We are fully poised, rested and connected to our internal Self, all of creation, and the cosmos. We are allied and supported in this dreamy state, trusting in the miracle soon to be given life. This is the festival of the QUEEN – of SELF-SOVEREIGNTY, ENTHRONEMENT, AND CROWNING of mind, body, and soul, of IDENTITY, of how we will incarnate in the coming year as Sacred Women. YULE is about our WISDOM AND GNOSIS. The Queen of Heaven and Holy Mother ensures that we use our mind and body in a symbiotic way as the Sun rebirths. We celebrate the active intellect, and our outward self-assertion returns.

The power of incubation and Gaia's darkness are gratefully honoured at this festival as the Sun returns. Our Queen is crowned and enthroned. We have Owl Wisdom – the deep knowing that everything changes, seasons come and go, day turns into night, night turns into day and birth always follows death. We have certainty, confidence, and comfort in all of this. The clarity of our 360-degree vision and absolute faith in our five senses, plus the miracle and sacredness of our embodiment, are vital at this festival as we wake up to the miracle of the union of mind, body, and spirit. This festival is about resting into the trust of our own truth and the paradoxical harmony of completion and change. Excitement can be sensed and yet we now know to pace ourselves and have faith in the intelligence of letting our body lead and bloom in its own time. Gestation and timings are Sacred. We KNOW there is a season and time for everything. We surrender into the trust and faith of the flow of grace.

Our ancestors deeply honoured the potency of the wheel and all it represented at this festival. At Yule, the wheel of time stops turning as Gaia completes her exhale – her release. There is a pause between breaths – the sacred space of anticipation and magic – the absence of everything, the dark cosmic and human womb of potentiality is all that remains – Sophia is here. We and Gaia then inhale again. Light conception happens and rebirth begins. The sun, daylight, and warmth return. The Virgin Mother Goddess rises.

There was great celebration in communities. Fires were lit and the Yule Log, usually of oak, the tree connected to the sun god, was burnt ritually, marking the oak king's triumph in the battle of the oak and holly kings at this solstice. The smoke from the log cleared the home from darker energies and blockages so the new energy could be invited in. Candles were a big part of this festival, also symbolising the return of life and the sun. This festival, as at Litha, merges polarity, simultaneously looking backwards and forwards, celebrating the full expansion of the inner, of darkness and death, whilst recognising the return of the outer, light and life. Our circular vision and step into timelessness as the wheel of the year pauses, frees us from the concept of linear time, and moves us into the eternal now. We receive the certainty that personal, ancestral and collective lines can be altered and changed at any given moment. We are constantly in Cerridwen's cauldron of regeneration in the dark half of the year and as Queen can be supported by any of the Goddess mentors to release, reconfigure and rebirth. We remember in our DNA what our ancestors revered and knew – that there is no differentiation between us and Gaia. We are the Triple Goddess; Virgin/Maiden in Spring, Lover/Mother/Warrioress in Summer, and Wisewoman/Crone in Winter and at Summer and Winter Solstice we are unified – Queen of Earth and Heaven – as one. We are all parts of Goddess, and how we express this is unique to us. It is our IDENTITY.

The homes of our ancestors were adorned with evergreens, such as holly, ivy, mistletoe, and the bows of sacred trees such as yew. The wheel was honoured by placing the evergreen wreaths on the door. There would be gatherings, candle lit processions and celebrations with carolling and feasting with lanterns and a table decoration honouring the wheel of the year and the four directions. Smoke was a symbol of the mystery of the phoenix rising and our ancestors would join with their family, in gratitude, dancing around the fires and bathing themselves in the smoke of the oak fires to smudge and cleanse their energy and physical form. There would be legend and storytelling and sharing throughout the night, dance and they would await and celebrate the sunrise, often making a commitment or intention or 'resolution' to ensure that the Light they have conceived is birthed into form.

This month we ask ourselves: *What are we conceiving? What blocks are keeping me from attaining my intentions – and what do I need to release? Conversely, we ask ourselves: What do I need to invite into my mind, body, energy to expand and make space for growth? What do I need more of? What needs to happen for me to follow and trust my 360-degree vision and wisdom?*

Our Owl is a symbol of the Lunar Feminine, of Wisdom, of intuition and our ability to see in the dark. Her circular vision means we can see completely – in all directions and perspectives – and then tune into our internal gnosis and truth to weigh it all up and decide what is right for us. She is a totem of midwifery and will support us in birthing that which we conceive with the grace and ease of her winged flight. In addition, the Owl helps us to connect to Awen, inspiration, and internal guidance – helping us see beyond illusion, masks, and deceit – and explore magic, change, and transitions with grace and ease. She is the faithful ally of the Queen and supports our self-sovereignty and the opening of SIGHT.

The ancient symbol of the crown is representative of authority, divinity, and sovereignty. It is the talisman of royalty, leadership, and dedication to service. The wearer is enthroned in their own wisdom and union with the Divine, the sacred marriage of heaven and earth, humanness, and divinity. The sanctity of womanhood. Crowns also symbolise glory, immortality, empowerment, and initiation. Stepping into the rulership of the Soul.

What a miracle a Sacred Woman is!

As at Litha, socialising, celebrating, and performing are activities of this month. Indoor fires further fuel our expression fires and joy. Love and gratitude for your community, singing and chanting together in union strengthens bonding. Making an altar, decorating with evergreens is a beautiful focus for working with intention setting. Lighting candles to invite the Light to kindle the flames of your desires is also a beautiful way of strengthening resilience and trust in cosmic support.

Most of all, we need to become focused and ensure our will is clearly aligned with our intentions and goals and that those we are in alliance with are serving our highest good and manifestation. This month is about cultivating and strengthening the power of the alignment of mind and body.

Take some time out to rest fully. Switch off. Have no agenda. Just be.

Tune into your nervous system. *What does it need from you this next year?* Set some intentions around inviting in calm, safety, and regulation around your daily practises.

At the festival of Yule, we connect with our QUEEN. We realise the POWER of GNOSIS and INTERNAL TRUTH and SELF-SOVEREIGNTY. We are everything and as such are VIRGIN, whole and holy unto SELF. Our body is the portal of MAGIC and MIRACLES.

Claiming Queendom, self-sovereignty, self-referencing, and self-leadership is a political act. You are free from the matrix and control of the external trends, paradigms, thoughts, advertising, and commercialism. You are whole and holy unto Your SELF. Your SELF gives your life meaning and Your SELF is your truth and identity. You complete yourself.

This piece is excerpted from Kay's workbook, *Mentorship with Goddess: Growing Sacred Womanhood,* published by Girl God Books in 2022.

Solstice Return to Light
Barbara O'Meara

Halcyon Times
Megha Morganfield

Halcyon times... calms the waves
As Solstice chimes,
      She calms the waves

Everything is turning,
      Everything is turning... everything

And her babes will rest
      in her watery nest

As her tender rays are born
As the light returns to her shore

Halcyon times... calms the waves
      She calms the waves

This is an original composition by Megha Morganfield. You can find it on her YouTube channel if you want to learn the tune.

I Will Set You Free
Cheryl Braganza

O Holy Night

Trista Hendren and Anders Løberg

O Holy Night! The stars are brightly shining,
It is the night that our Goddess returns;
Long lay the world in suffering and oppression—
'Til She appears and we all feel our worth.
A thrill of hope, the weary world rejoices,
For yonder breaks, a new and glorious morn;

Rise from your knees,
Oh, hear the women's power!
O night divine, O night when Goddess rose
O night, divine, O night, O night divine.

Truly She taught us to love one another;
Her way is love and Her gospel is peace;
Chains shall She break, the slave is no longer
And in Her name all oppression shall cease.
Sweet hymns of joy, orgasmic chorus raise Her,
Let all within us praise Her holy name;
She reigns on high
Oh, praise Her name forever!
Her strength and love, Her strength and her love,
O night, O night divine, O night divine.

O Holy Night! The stars are brightly shining,
It is the night that our Goddess Returns;
Long lay the world in suffering and oppression—
'Til She appears and we all felt our worth.
A thrill of hope the weary world rejoices,
For yonder breaks a new and glorious morn;

Rise from your knees,
Oh, hear the women's power!
O night divine, O night when Goddess rose
O night, divine, O night, O night divine.

Oh Holy Dawn
Dale Allen

Oh holy dawn
The sun is surely rising.
It is the morn of the Goddess' return

Born in us all
She holds all life as sacred
Our hearts rejoice in remembering

Her body is the earth and all creation
All life is free to thrive in peace and joy.

Rise to your feet
Oh hear the ancient voices!
Oh love within

Feel Her strength and love within.
Oh love di-VINE
Oh love Her love divine.

Star Catcher
Sue Ellen Parkinson

Winter Goddess Comes Alive In Me
(Sung to *The Holly and the Ivy*)
Dr Lynne Sedgmore

The forest shines and glitters
With newly fallen snow.
I feel the stillness, hear the quiet.
And then I see the doe.

In the presence of the deer
And the innocence she brings
Winter Goddess comes alive in me
My heart rejoicing sings.

The doe comes close, then closer,
Our eyes meet face to face,
A beautiful exchange of love,
Precious moment filled with grace.

In the presence of the deer
And the innocence she brings
Winter Goddess comes alive in me
My heart rejoicing sings.

I walk amongst the trees
Touched by the deer's display.
I stop within a spacious glade,
I bow and start to pray.

Through the presence of the deer
And the innocence she brings
Winter Goddess comes alive in me
My heart rejoicing sings.

The sacredness of life
On this winter solstice morn
Enlivens every leaf and tree
Every living thing reborn.

Through the presence of the deer
And the innocence she brings
Winter Goddess comes alive in me
My heart rejoicing sings.

The forest shines and glitters
With newly fallen snow.
I feel the stillness, hear the quiet,
I have seen the sacred doe.

Through the presence of the deer
And the innocence she brings
Winter Goddess comes alive in me
My heart rejoicing sings.

The Holly & the Ivy
Chelsea Arrington

I.
The holly and the ivy,
When they are both full grown,
Of all the trees that are in the wood,
The holly bears the crown.

~Chorus~

O the rising of the Sun
And the running of the deer,
The playing of the merry pipes,
Sweet singing of the fey.

II.
The holly bears a blossom
As white as lily flower
And the Mother births bright Solstice Sun
To give us strength and power.

~Chorus~

III.
The holly bears a berry
As red as any blood
And the Mother births bright Solstice Sun
To make our days bright and good.

~Chorus~

IV.
The holly bears a prickle
As sharp as any thorn
And the Mother births bright Solstice Sun
On Midwinter morn.

~Chorus~

V.
The holly bears a bark
As bitter as any gall
And the Mother births bright Solstice Sun
To make Spring come for all.

~Chorus~

VI.
The holly and the ivy!
Now both are full well grown.
Of all the trees that are in the wood,
The holly bears the crown.

~Chorus~

Glorious Goddess
(Sung to *Ave Maria*)
Anique Duc Radiant Heart

Glorious Goddess
Blessed are we to know your love
Each day and in every waking moment
Our hearts are lifted by your grace
Glorious One, in you we find our truth
And we are transformed

In a world where there is pain and suffering
You teach us to focus on the good
With your light you gently point the way
To our place of bliss that lies with you
Glorious Goddess………………………..

Glorious Goddess
Teach us to know your love
To push aside our doubts and fears
To live our lives in the now
Glorious One, help us to know your gifts
That we may be transformed

To serve you in your temple
Is all we ever ask of you
May you guide our words and our deeds
As we craft a better world with you
Glorious Goddess……………………..

Glorious Goddess
Grateful are we to know your love
To know that with every sacred breath
We fill the world with your grace
Glorious One, in you we find our peace
And we are transformed
To stand strong in our service
In your presence ever more
We live to sing your praises
To feel the warmth of your violet light

Glorious Goddess... Glorious Goddess...

I am a Goddess
Kat Shaw

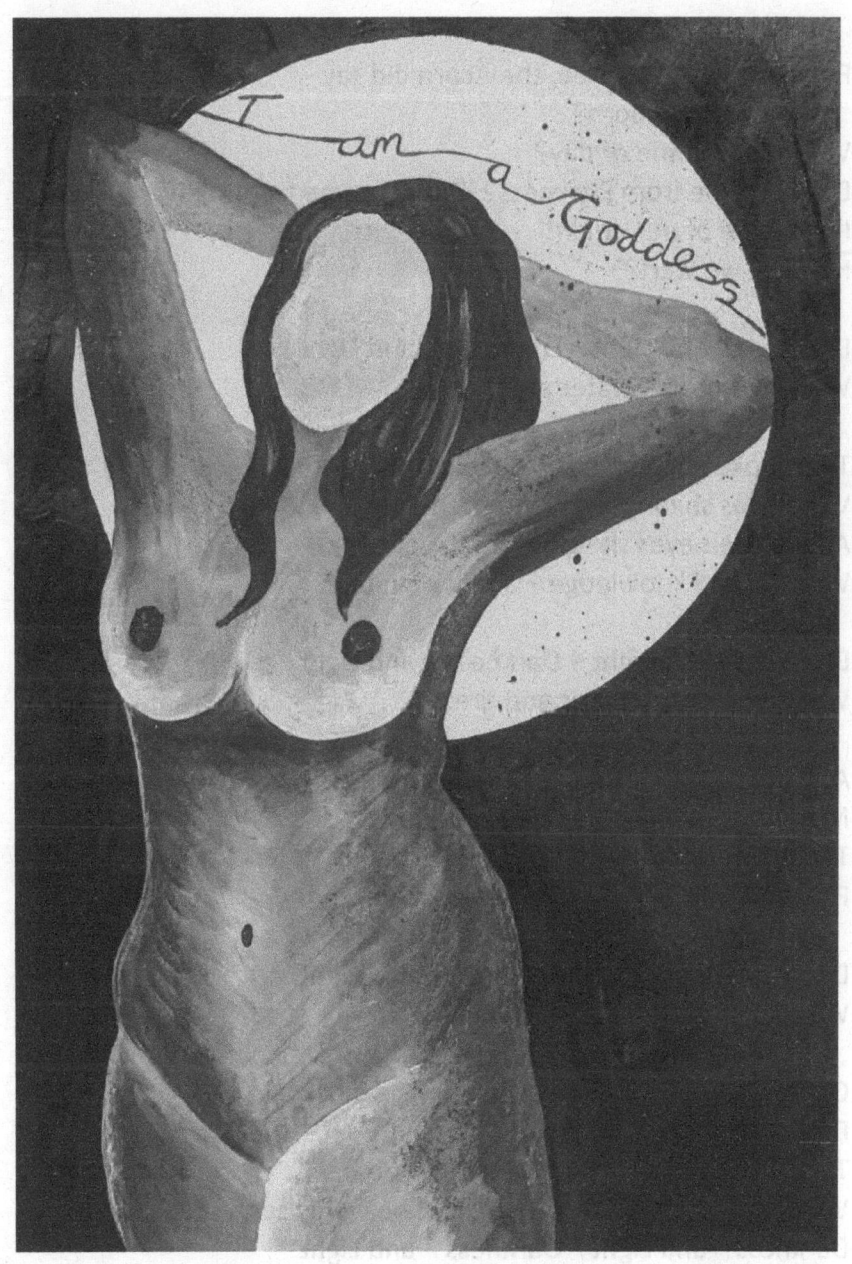

From the First Oak Tree, the Acorn Did Say
(Sung to *The First Noel*)
Kay Louise Aldred

From the First Oak Tree, the Acorn did say
'When were we born?
Was it night-time or day?
Did we come from Darkness? Did we come from Light?
I'm unsure of our origin!
How did we start?'

Darkness – and Light – Darkness – and Light
We are of both – water and fire.

They looked up and saw The Star,
Venus was shining – beyond them far,
And to their eyes she gave great Sight,
Wisdom and knowledge – a quick ignite.

Darkness – and Light – Darkness – and Light
We are of both – water and fire.

And by the Light of that same Star
Memories of origin flooded them fast,
The original pulse with a negative charge
Filled by an electric bolt that was large.

Darkness – and Light – Darkness – and Light
We are of both – water and fire.

Conception of the Light – the building block laid
Evolving Life to the present day,
The Acorn recognised her ancestral descent
Was the whole Universe – she was heavenly sent.
Darkness – and Light – Darkness – and Light
We are of both – water and fire.

Máthair agus Leanabh'
Barbara O'Meara

The Winter Solstice Carol

(Sung to *The Coventry Carol: Lullay, Thou Little Tiny Child*)

Sharon Smith

1. Come now, My Daughters, hear my Call
Winter is here to stay;
O, Come, My Daughters, One and All
Celebrate Solstice Day.

2. O Sisters, too, we call to you,
Light now the Yule Logs bright;
And Dance and Sing, your Gifts to bring
On Winter Solstice Night.

3. And Mothers, all, the time has come,
Bring forth your children dear;
And teach them of this holy time,
Longest night of the year.

4. When Goddess births the Sun anew,
Oak King regains his power;
As light and warmth return to Earth
After this Solstice hour.

5. But for this day the Darkness reigns,
Lie now against Her breast;
She will enfold you in Her arms
And bring you blessed rest.

6. Gather, my Daughters, one and all,
Welcome the coming Light;
With voices raised in revelry
On Winter Solstice Night.

The Darkest Night Enfolds Us Here

(Sung to *O Come, O Come, Immanuel*)

Rebekah Myers

The darkest night enfolds us here
The deepest darkness of the year
We wait for the return of the light
A spark of hope throughout the winter night

O come, O come
We call to you as one
Return to us, beloved Sun

O Lady bright with power, Queen of all
We plead with you to heed our fervent call
As you have birthed the Sun anew
May we rebirth ourselves to walk with you

O come, O come
We call to you as one
Return to us, beloved Sun

Copyright © by Rebekah Myers, December 20, 2020

Winter Queen
Jassy Watson

Once in Chaos, Primordial Creation

(Sung to *Once in Royal David's City*)

Kay Louise Aldred

Once in Chaos, Primordial Creation,
Tiamat rose, 'the glistening one'!
This Creatrix Dragon Mother,
Birthed as Serpent of the seas.
Tiamat was the Goddess wild,
Offering existence tempered and mild.

She formed heaven and earth from water,
Sacred parent, we're enthralled.
Dark and Light, deity and human,
She births encompassing all.
Havoc! Mayhem! Disarray!
Building blocks of night and day.

Also named a Rainbow Serpent,
Dragons of creation myths.
Bridging earth and heaven stealthily,
Finding water – a blessed gift!
Shedding skins, to birth anew,
Knowledge and instinct, they grew and grew.

Dragon Goddess still sustains us,
Through the Ley Lines, Gaia's blood.
Lifeforce energy flows so freely,
Creatures track to find their food.
Ancient pathways underground,
Life sustaining, pulsing and unbound.

Spinning the Sun
Cheryl Braganza

Spiral to the Centre
(Sung to *Away in the Manger*)

Kay Louise Aldred

Spiral to the centre
To Earth's deepest core
Gaia is ready
To tell the folklore

The Queen of the Underworld
Is waiting for us
To discard all our masks
And to give up on fuss

Status means nothing
When we're totally bare
When there's nowhere to hide
From Ereshkigal's stare

Courage! Hold steady!
In devotion to Light
And let the Great Goddess
Give us exit from night

Move back through the darkness
Push through lifeless soil
Rebirth in innocence
Divine-Golden-Child

Mothered by Goddess
We know we remain
Embraced in her arms
And loved in all ways

As her dear children
She extends us fierce care
The gates of the darkness
Are nothing to fear!

Three Graces
Cheryl Braganza

I Heard the Bells on Solstice Morn
(Sung to *I Heard The Bells On Christmas Day*)
Trista Hendren

I heard the bells on Solstice morn[24]
Their ancient melodies ring on
And wild and sweet their songs repeat
Of peace on Earth, good will to all

I grieved that we have lost so much
Patriarchy took too much
It forced along the broken song
Of war on Earth, good will to none

In despair, I bowed my head
There is no peace on earth, I said
For hate is strong and mocks the song
Of peace on Earth, good will to all

Then pealed the bells, more loud and deep
She is not dead, nor does She sleep
We'll right all wrongs and sing Her songs
Of peace on Earth, good will to all

---

[24] According to *The Woman's Dictionary of Symbols & Sacred Objects* by Barbara G. Walker: "Bells have always been associated with mystical happenings and communication with spirits. Goddess images in the shape of bells are known from very ancient times." (from Chapter 7: Secular-Sacred Objects).

This song in its original form was written on Christmas Day in 1863 by American poet Henry Wadsworth Longfellow. Two years earlier, his wife tragically burned to death, and he was badly burned as he tried to save her. On top of this, his son had been wounded in the Civil War and was temporarily paralyzed. Longfellow was so torn apart by all of this that he worried he would be institutionalized.

I have always thought it was a beautiful song, but I did not know the story behind it. The God language didn't sit right with me over time. However, a lot of the words, sadly, still ring very true – and I left many of them in place. The third stanza is almost entirely original as it does not seem we have learned anything about creating and maintaining peace on Earth.

I began working on this song the night before I heard about the tragic murder of the Singh Sikh family in California. I started sobbing at breakfast thinking about the beautiful 8-month-old girl child, Aroohi, who was left to die alone at the base of an almond tree. I pray that the Tree held her through the terror of her last days.

I dedicate this song to her memory.

The Blessing
Sue Ellen Parkinson

All Life is This, Who at the Breast

(Sung to *What Child is This*)

Kay Louise Aldred

All Life is this, who at the breast
Of Mother's body, are feeding?
Whom Gaia greets with her sustenance sweet
Whilst nature spirits watch keeping.

This, this is humanity
Whom Goddess nurtures so all things be,
Quick, quick, awaken now
To Gaia's body with reverence.

See how we live in abundant flow
Where Gaia's body is flourishing,
Let all be freed from scarcity
Receiving copious nourishing.

Plants, greening, inspire us all
To plant and sow – to reap and share,
Hail, Goddess, the seed of life
Primordial force of cosmos!

So clean her waters, all rivers, seas,
Come clear your home of pollutants.
Grow vegetables for your family,
Share plenty at this Solstice.

Raise, raise, your songs of joy,
To Gaia in her slumbering,
Joy, joy, and Solstice cheer,
Maiden, Mother and Crone!

Snow Angel
Cheryl Braganza

It Came Upon a Solstice Morn

(Sung to *It Came Upon a Midnight Clear*)

Carol P. Christ

It came upon a Solstice morn,
that glorious song of old,
with angels bending near the earth,
to touch their harps of gold.

"Peace on the earth.
good will to all,"
from heaven's all glorious realm.
The world in silent stillness waits,
to hear the angels sing.

I wake (in) the dark of Solstice morn.
Mountains shrouded in clouds,
cold wind blowing,
light dawns.

My mother heard
the angels sing,
on Solstice eve,
calling me to life,
her Christmas Carol.

Blessed Mother Always With Us.

Longing for my beloved,
on Solstice morn,
I heard Sappho sing:
Thank you, my dear
You came and you did
well to come: I needed
you. You have made
love blaze up in
my breast—bless you!
Bless you as often
as the hours have
been endless to me
when you were gone.

Cold tiles,
bare feet,
coffee brewing,
elderly dog stirring,
I open the garden door.

And there it is.
Solstice miracle.
Three purple irises.
blooming in the cold.
Life triumphing over death,
every time.

Originally shared on *Feminism and Religion* on December 25, 2017. Shared with their permission.

Notes from Carol P. Christ:

Sappho translated by Mary Barnard.

Thanks to Miriam Robbins Dexter for digging iris bulbs from her garden for me to plant in mine.

My mother promised my father to name me Susan or Peter but when she heard carolers in the hospital, she changed her mind.

Note from Trista:

We were never able to sing this in its entirety as it was written. Rebekah Myers read it as a poem at our first Solstice Sing-along in 2021. We have included Megha Morganfield's version on the next page for your singing enjoyment!

It Came Upon a Midnight Clear
Megha Morganfield

It came upon a midnight clear
That glorious song of old
From strong heard voices on the earth
That warmed us in the cold
Peace on the earth, good will to all
To heaven and earth we bring
The message through the ages
Let peace come as we sing

The night with crystal air is filled
The words so crystal clear
To hold the highest need for all
That peace is the most dear
As we gather strength and love
The message will resound
For every heart must hold to this
That peace must be found

And so we sing this anthem song
Abiding in the faith
That our intentions will ring true
A new world to awake
Where peace leads to all harmony
And peace the sweet renewed
The victory is lost to love
As peace is what we choose
As peace is what we choose

The Pale Winter Sunlight
(Sung to *I Wonder as I Wander*)

Rebekah Myers

The pale winter sunlight
sinks low in the sky.
A snowflake falls gently,
December's soft sigh.
A candle glows clearly
through window nearby.
I wonder and wander –
beneath winter's sky.

I pause and I ponder
in winter's dark womb.
I rest and I dream
In the snow-covered gloom.
This time of gestation;
the promise of bloom.
I dream and I ponder –
In Mother Earth's womb

We light our bonfires
as we sing up the Sun.
We wait for the light
as we welcome the One,
as lo, o'er the mountain
the first rays appear,
the light is returning –
To greet a new year.

Copyright © by Rebekah Myers, December 9th, 2021

Women of the World Unite
Cheryl Braganza

Your Love Heals All Our Wounding
(Sung to *O Come All Ye Faithful*)

Dr. Lynne Sedgmore

We sing, we who love you, happy and ecstatic
We come home, we come home, feel Mother's embrace
Standing before you
Joyfully singing
Your love heals all our wounding
Your love heals all our wounding
Your love heals all our wounding
Goddess divine

Dark and light, blood of life
We all are born from our mother's womb
Mighty Creatrix
Birther of potential
Your love heals all our wounding
Your love heals all our wounding
Your love heals all our wounding
Goddess divine

Singing like angels, happily rejoicing
Offr'ing our gratitude for blessing received
Glorious Goddess
Joyfully we praise you
Your love heals all our wounding
Your love heals all our wounding
Your love heals all our wounding
Goddess divine

Goddess we love you, hearts and minds wide open
Bringing to you, all that we are
Power of our Mother
Liberates and strengthens
Your love heals all our wounding
Your love heals all our wounding
Your love heals all our wounding
Goddess divine

Home
Barbara O'Meara

Bring A Torch And Light The Watch Fires
(Sung to *Bring A Torch, Jeanette, Isabella*)
Deborah A. Meyerriecks

In the sky, the Sun took its station,
In the sky, see the Sun has gone.
In the dark, we'll wait in silence
Think now back on all we've done
Ah! ah! Shorter has been the daylight
Ah! ah! Long now has grown the night.

Bring a torch and light the watch fires
Bring a torch, and all of us come.
Sun is setting, the longest night starting;
Day is done, longest night's begun.
Ah! Shorter has been the daylight
Ah! ah! Longer has grown the night

Quiet now, we wait in the darkness,
Seeking wisdom to know ourselves.
In the dark, we'll divine inspiration;
Lessons past and still some left to learn.
Ah, listen the night wind whispers,
Ah, ah, find your tranquility.

With the sunrise, a new year emerges.
Soft the glow of the new born sun.
New year dawning, so bright with potential
Catch the sparks; ignite our flames
As we step forth into a new day
With lessons learned on Solstice Night.

Three Queens
Barbara O'Meara

We Sing in Deepest, Darkest Night
(Sung to *Three Kings from Persian Lands Afar*)
Kay Louise Aldred

We sing in deepest, darkest, night
Evoking the returning Light:
And this the quest of the revellers be,
Where oh where? The new-born sun may be!
The evergreens hold us within Life:
Fire, candles, Yule log – are our offerings.

The stars shine down with steadfast rays
Joined in our celebratory games,
With pleasure, laughter and sacred sound,
We together sing our blessed rounds!
We praise-give with our collective voice
Breath, music, joy – are our offerings.

A moment paused and the great stand still!
A recalibrating! Be with the nil!
A moment nothing, a moment all,
Shall lead our hearts to collective call.
Hate, greed, divide we will not bring
Into the Light, as the wheel turns again –
We begin to sing.

PaGaian Joy to the World
Glenys Livingstone PhD

Joy to the World
The light returns
Let All receive Her Love

CHORUS:
Let every Heart
Let every tongue
Repeat the sounding Joy
Repeat the sounding Joy
Let Creatures, and all of Nature sing

She moves the stars
With Her Desire[25]
Let All receive Her Power

CHORUS

She grows the seed
With all Her Love
Let All receive Her Wisdom

CHORUS

She lights our Hearts
She grows our food
Let All receive Her Joy

CHORUS

---

[25] In the original paper version of the book the word "might" is used. Upon further thought, I preferred the metaphor of Desire.

Joy to the World
The Light returns
Let All receive Her Love

(From the Winter Solstice ritual referred to in Chapter 7 of PaGaian Cosmology*)*

Purnima[26]
Cheryl Braganza

---

[26] Note from Cheryl: Purnima/Full Moon (in Sanskrit) is my poetic and colorful evocation of the celebration of women worldwide through dance and music. The Purnima dance was originally inspired by the devadasis (courtesans) of early modern South India, signifying love, longing and desire. It evolved into the present Bharatnatyam form. My favourite Goethe quote spirals through the dancers "Rest not; life is sweeping by. Go dare before you die. Something mighty & sublime, leave behind to conquer time".

Joy to the World
Alissa DeLaFuente

Joy to the world, the Crone has come!
Let earth perceive her Truth;
Let every heart prepare Her room.
Let neighbors and sisters see,
Let brothers and kings see,
Let mountain, and ocean, and valley see.

Joy to the earth, the Maiden speaks!
Let earth perceive her Voice;
Let women sing her songs, let all sing her songs,
Repeat the sounding joy,
Repeat the sounding joy,
Repeat, repeat the sounding joy.

Joy to the world, the Mother sings!
Let us join her in song.
May we celebrate and love, nurture and create,
Root ourselves in love,
Root ourselves in love,
Root the world in radical love.

The moon waxes, is full, and wanes;
The movement of our lives.
The shadows and the joy, the pain and circumstance,
And yet still we sing,
And yet still we sing,
And yet, for love and joy, we sing.

Voices We Have Heard on High

(Sung to *Angels We Have Heard on High*)

Megha Morganfield

Voices we have heard on high,
Sweetly singing o'er the plains
And the mountains in reply
Echoing our joyful strains
Gloria, we sing oh so merrily
Gloria, we sing oh so merrily

People why this jubilee
Why your heart felt strains prolong
What the gladsome tidings be
That inspired your heavenly song
Gloria, we sing of so merrily
Gloria, we sing oh so merrily

With friends and kindred spirits here
These Yuletide songs bring us near
We are filled with happiness
Moments are so full of bliss
Gloria, we sing of so merrily
Gloria, we sing oh so merrily

The Crone Has Come!
Andrea Redmond

We Sing Her Creation Story

(Sung to *Gloria aka Iris – Angels from the Realms of Glory*)

Dr Lynne Sedgmore

We sing Her creation story
Spread Her joy across the earth
Know Her darkness and Her glory
Winter Solstice deep rebirth
Creatrix
Blessings on this Yuletime
Creatrix
Blessings on this Yuletime

She breathes life into all beings
Shines the moon and spreads white snow
Web of life refreshed and freeing
Feel the festive cheer and glow
Creatrix
Blessings on this Yuletime
Creatrix
Blessings on this Yuletime

All creation, join our singing
Winter time of ice and cold
Feel the tingle She is bringing
Loudly sing, your voices bold
Creatrix
Blessings on this Yuletime
Creatrix
Blessings on this Yuletime

Transformation through Her cycles
Birth, decay, death and rebirth
Warp and weft, circles and spirals
Life enhancing Goddess mirth
Creatrix
Blessings on this Yuletime
Creatrix
Blessings on this Yuletime

We sing Her creation story
Spread Her joy across the earth
Know Her darkness and Her glory
Winter Solstice deep rebirth
Creatrix
Blessings on this Yuletime
Creatrix
Blessings on this Yuletime

Oh Mother Earth Our Sacred Home
(Sung to *Oh Little Town of Bethlehem*)
Megha Morganfield

O Mother Earth our sacred home,
    how still we see you lie
Above your deep and dreamless sleep
    the silent stars go by
And in their soothing vigil,
    our mortal life is twined
For as they bring hope in the night
    our inner light does shine.

To rid ourselves of evil
    we must become like stars
That light the path for truth seekers
    so we will all go far
The light we share with others
    comes back into our souls
So when we're shining in the night,
    the darkness can't be cold

How silently, how silently,
    the night passes away
So soon the sun will rise again
    to herald a new day
How full of life all will become,
    because the sun does shine
And we part of the brightness
    magnify the divine

O Girl Child of the Great Goddess

(Sung to *O Little Town of Bethlehem*)

Kay Louise Aldred

O Girl Child of the Great Goddess,
how still we see you lie
Above thy deep and fae-filled sleep,
the silent stars go by.
Within our hearts you shineth,
as everlasting Light
The hopes and dreams of all earth's beings,
beam bright as you tonight.

How silently, how silently,
The wondrous gift is seen
Girl Child imparts within our hearts,
The blessings of her heaven
Life and joy and wonderment,
Creative spark within
Her wholeness will completely fill
Us up with powerful will!

O Girl Child, Solar Feminine
Expand in us! we say,
Empower us! Shout! Jiggle us all about
Turn us on – everyday,
We hear the songs of Angels
Singing sunshine into form,
To manifest, as her – that's best
The Holy Girl God formed.

Yule Girl
Andrea Redmond

Cosmic Silent Night for Winter Solstice

Connie Barlow

Silent night. Holy night. All is calm. All is bright.
PLAN-ets GRACE-ful-ly CIR-cle the SUN
STAR-dust CY-cles through EV-er-y ONE
Life abounds upon Earth. Life abounds upon Earth.

Silent night. Holy night. All is calm. All is bright.
RA-di-ant BEAMS from PRI-mor-dial STARS
CLUMPED in-to PLAN-ets like VE-nus and MARS
Life abounds upon Earth. Life abounds upon Earth.

Silent night. Holy night. All is calm. All is bright.
CAR-bon NI-tro-gen AND cal-ci-UM
ALL were BORN in-side AN-ces-tral SUNS
Life abounds upon Earth. Life abounds upon Earth.

Silent night. Holy night. All is calm. All is bright.
DEATH and re-CY-cling of MILL-ions of STARS
BROUGHT forth PLAN-ets and ALL that we ARE
Life abounds upon Earth. Life abounds upon Earth.

Silent night. Holy night. All is calm. All is bright.
SIL-ver GOLD and TI-ta-ni-UM
FORGED in STARS be-fore EARTH had be-GUN
Life abounds upon Earth. Life abounds upon Earth.

Silent night. Holy night. All is calm. All is bright.
FLAR-ing FORTH a-cross HEAV-en a-BOVE
SU-per-NO-vas made ALL that we LOVE
Life abounds upon Earth. Life abounds upon Earth.

NOTE: This "stardust" version of Silent Night was first used by Connie at the December 21, 2003, intergenerational Sunday service of the Unitarian Universalist Fellowship of Clemson, South Carolina.

All is One
Barbara O'Meara

To Folks and Friends
(Sung to *God Rest Ye Merry Gentlemen*)
Megha Morganfield

Oh rest ye merry folks and friends
    let nothing you dismay
There's so much to be joyful for
    in nature's great display
That if you let go of the past
    there's creation every day

Yes, tidings of comfort and joy,
    comfort and joy
Yes, tidings of comfort and joy.

So fill your lungs with Winter air
    and lift your head in awe
This is your world this is your life
    so let your spirits thaw
To hear these words that ring so true
    and let them be your call

Yes, tidings of comfort and joy,
    comfort and joy
Yes, tidings of comfort and joy.

For as the solstice holds our faith
    within the season's song
And as another cycle starts
    so have you just begun
And with this offer warm yourself
    let love the fire spawn

Yes, tidings of comfort and joy,
    comfort and joy
Yes, tidings of comfort and joy.

Hark, The Time Has Come to Sing
(Sung to *Hark, The Herald Angels Sing*)
Megha Morganfield

Hark the time has come to sing,
    glory is in everything
Peace on earth, let live within,
    this we strive to have begin
Joyful words that lift our spirits,
    bring to all so they may hear it
We are freed by our proclaim,
    life divine, deserves new fame
Hark the time has come to sing,
    glory is in everything

Shining sun above adored,
    humbled by the meaning forged
Born we here upon the earth,
    part of the constant rebirth
By divine chance we're alive
    glory to the mystery tide
Suffer not in pain or guilt
    life's meaning is what you will
Hark the time has come to sing,
    glory is in everything.

Prayers and soothing adulations,
    herald all creation
Carols ring into the darkness,
    as we sing unto the blest
Never alone in truth now gleaning,
    what's done is done...
    a new beginning
Love all first and set them free,
    some say yes... "let it be"
Hark the time has come to sing,
    glory is in everything

Yule Crone
Andrea Redmond

Go Tell It On The Mountain

Trista Hendren

Go, tell it on the mountain
Over the hills and everywhere
Go, tell it on the mountain
That Goddess DID come first!

While Grandmas kept their watching
O'er precious babes by night
Behold throughout the heavens
There shone a Holy light

Go, tell it on the mountain
Over the hills and everywhere
Go, tell it on the mountain
That Goddess DID come first!

The patriarchy trembled
When, lo! Upon the Earth
A Gulabi Gang of Warriors
Reminded who gave birth

Go, tell it on the mountain
Over the hills and everywhere
Go, tell it on the mountain
That Goddess DID come first!

Upon a grassy hilltop
A tiny girl was born
She gave us love and freedom
That blessed Solstice morn

Go, tell it on the mountain
Over the hills and everywhere
Go, tell it on the mountain
That Goddess DID come first!
That Goddess DID come first!

Trim the Halls
(Sung to *Deck the Halls*)
Sharon Smith

Trim the halls with boughs of holly,
Fa-la-la-la-la, la-la-la-la!
Solstice time is here, by golly!
Fa-la-la-la-la, la-la-la-la!
On the hearth, the Yule Log blazing,
Fa-la-la, la-la-la, la-la-la!
Gratitude, our voices raising,
Fa-la-la-la-la, la-la-la-la!

On the stove the Wassail sim'ring,
Fa-la-la-la-la, la-la-la-la!
In the windows, candles glim'ring
Fa-la-la-la-la, la-la-la-la!
Longest night in all the year,
Fa-la-la, la-la-la, la-la-la!
Join me now in Solstice cheer,
Fa-la-la-la-la, la-la-la-la!

Now the Oak King's strength is growing,
Fa-la-la-la-la, la-la-la-la!
While the wintry winds are blowing,
Fa-la-la-la-la, la-la-la-la!
Wheel of Seasons ever-turning,
Fa-la-la, la-la-la, la-la-la!
While the Yule Log's brightly burning,
Fa-la-la-la-la, la-la-la-la!

Lift the Wassail, lads and lasses,
Fa-la-la-la-la, la-la-la-la!
Joyful as the old year passes!
Fa-la-la-la-la, la-la-la-la!
Hail the new year now before us,
Fa-la-la, la-la-la, la-la-la!
As we sing a Solstice chorus,
Fa-la-la-la-la, la-la-la-la!

Solstice Night

(Sung to *Jingle Bells*)
Sharon Smith

Winter Solstice time
Is upon us once again,
Gather loved ones near
Give thanks for what has been

Seasons cycle by
Summer turns to Fall
And Harvest time is plentiful
Give thanks now, One and All!

Oh,

Bonfire bright, Solstice Night,
Longest of the year,
Gather with your kith and kin
And have yourselves some cheer

Hey!

Bonfire bright, Solstice Night,
Longest of the year,
Gather with your kith and kin
And have yourself some cheer!

Dark defeats the Light,
And Holly bows to Oak,
But on this sacred night,
The Goddess does invoke

The turning of the Wheel
So daylight will return,
Now circle up your family
And watch the Bonfire burn!

Oh,

Bonfire bright, Solstice Night,
Longest of the year,
Gather with your kith and kin
And have yourself some cheer,

Hey!

Bonfire bright, Solstice Night,
Longest of the year,
Gather with your kith and kin
And have yourself some cheer!
Gather with your kith and kin
And have yourself some cheer!

Spirit of Dawn
Sue Ellen Parkinson

Arc of Stars

(Sung to *Boston*, an American Christmas hymn)

Claire Dorey

A hymn to honour the Ancient Egyptian Sky Goddess Nuit, also known as Nut and Nwt, as She arches over humanity.

She rises. Starry Nuit
Arching across the sky
A Ce-les-ti-al De-i-ty
Oh Cosmic Mother why
Were you lost and obscured from me?
Cow Goddess. Soaring high
How you nourish humanity
Gentle soul. Maternal eye

Mother of cycles, night to day
Her colour indigo
Full moon. Star light. Golden sunray
Shine on Earth. Saffron glow
Radiant as the Milky Way
As water, so stars flow
Rain and tears are poetry She says
As above so below

Rise up pyra-mid into focus
Earth. Sky. From rivers flood
Divine trance. Per-fume. Blue Lotus
Sacred as mother's blood
Creative wisdom. Divine Opus
Con-scious-ness born from mud
Stars and heavens dance within us
Cosmos flows. Ideas bud

Come sisters sing Her healing song
Summon with the sistrum
Nuit says we can all come along
Dance be free. Sing or hum
Together we are truly strong
Arc of stars. Crown of sun
Claim the rythmic sky. We belong
Cosmic heart. Earth beat drum

Goddess of Galactic Balance
Kat Shaw

The Twelve Days of Solstice

Margi Curtis

1. On the first day of Solstice the Goddess gave to me
    a pentacle upon the Goddess Tree.

2. On the second day of Solstice the Goddess gave to me
    two pointy hats
    and a pentacle upon the Goddess Tree.

3. On the third day of Solstice the Goddess gave to me
    three cauldron legs,
    two pointy hats
    and a pentacle upon the Goddess Tree.

4. On the fourth day of Solstice the Goddess gave to me
    four quarters-calling,
    three cauldron legs,
    two pointy hats
    and a pentacle upon the Goddess Tree.

5. On the fifth day of Solstice the Goddess gave to me
    FIVE El-e-ments,
    four quarters-calling,
    three cauldron legs,
    two pointy hats
    and a pentacle upon the Goddess Tree.

6. On the sixth day of Solstice the Goddess gave to me
    six Tarot readings,
    FIVE Elements,
    four quarters-calling,
    three cauldron legs,
    two pointy hats
    and a pentacle upon the Goddess Tree.

7. On the seventh day of Solstice the Goddess gave to me
   seven Chakras spinning,
   six Tarot readings,
   FIVE Elements,
   four quarters-calling,
   three cauldron legs,
   two pointy hats
   and a pentacle upon the Goddess Tree.

8. On the eighth day of Solstice the Goddess gave to me
   eight Seasons Feasting,
   seven Chakras spinning,
   six Tarot readings,
   FIVE Elements,
   four quarters-calling,
   three cauldron legs, two pointy hats,
   and a pentacle upon the Goddess Tree.

9. On the ninth day of Solstice the Goddess gave to me
   nine Muses musing,
   eight Seasons Feasting,
   seven Chakras spinning,
   six Tarot readings,
   FIVE Elements,
   four quarters-calling,
   three cauldron legs,
   two pointy hats,
   and a pentacle upon the Goddess Tree.

10. On the tenth day of Solstice the Goddess gave to me
    ten fingers twinkling
    nine Muses musing,
    eight Seasons Feasting,
    seven Chakras spinning,
    six Tarot readings,
    FIVE Elements,
    four quarters-calling,
    three cauldron legs,
    two pointy hats,
    and a pentacle upon the Goddess Tree.

11. On the eleventh day of Solstice the Goddess gave to me
    eleven Full Moon Meetings,
    ten fingers twinkling
    nine Muses musing,
    eight Seasons Feasting,
    seven Chakras spinning,
    six Tarot readings,
    FIVE Elements,
    four quarters-calling,
    three cauldron legs,
    two pointy hats,
    and a pentacle upon the Goddess Tree.

12. On the twelfth day of Solstice the Goddess gave to me
    twelve Star Signs beaming,
    eleven Full Moon meetings,
    ten fingers twinkling
    nine Muses musing,
    eight Seasons feasting,
    seven Chakras spinning,
    six Tarot readings,
    FIVE Elements,
    four quarters-calling,
    three cauldron legs,
    two pointy hats,
    and a pentacle upon the Goddess Tree.

Winter Solstice Day is Here
(Sung to *Jolly Old Saint Nicholas*)
Sharon Smith

Winter Solstice Day is here,
Let us now begin;
Bring the Yule Log to the hearth,
Welcome kith and kin.

Orange pomanders in a bowl,
Wassail in the pot;
Table spread with Solstice fare,
Blessings for the lot.

Light the candles 'round the house,
Bask now in their glow.
Lift your voice in merry song,
Let your praises flow.

For the longer days return,
Bringing back the Sun;
Time to let the old things go,
New cycle has begun.

When the darkness settles in
Stars light up the night,
Hasten to the Bonfire now
Let the blaze burn bright.

Share your joy with one and all
And your Solstice cheer;
Grateful for this Sacred Day,
The shortest of the year.

Bus Stop
Cheryl Braganza

Light We Now the Solstice Fire with We Wish You a Blessed Solstice

(Sung to *Here We Come A-caroling* and
We Wish You a Merry Christmas)

Sharon Smith

Light we now the Solstice Fire,
And string the Evergreen!
And Holly bright with berries,
So fair to be seen!
Love and joy come to you,
And to you glad Solstice too,
Goddess bless you and send you,
A Happy New Year,
Goddess send you a Happy New Year!

Spread now Solstice Greetings,
Among your kith and kin!
Be the friendly neighbors,
Whom others will let in!
Love and joy come to you,
And to you glad Solstice too,
Goddess bless you and send you,
A Happy New Year,
Goddess send you a Happy New Year!

Goddess bless our loving homes,
And all who dwell within;
Mothers, Fathers, Children
And all our closest kin;
"Love and joy!" be our cry,
Lift our mugs of wassail high;
Goddess bless us and send us a Happy New Year,
Goddess send us a Happy New Year.

To all our kin and kinsfolk
That dwell both far and near,
We wish you Happy Solstice
And a Blessed New Year.
"Love and joy!" be our cry,
Lift our mugs of wassail high;
Goddess bless us and send us a Happy New Year,
Goddess send us a Happy New Year.

We wish you a Blessed Solstice,
We wish you a Blessed Solstice,
We wish you a Blessed Solstice,
And a Happy New Year!
Good tidings to you,
Wherever you are,
Good tidings for Solstice,
And a Happy New Year!

We wish you a Blessed Solstice,
We wish you a Blessed Solstice,
We wish you a Blessed Solstice,
And a Happy New Year!

We wish you a Blessed Solstice,
We wish you a Blessed Solstice,
We wish you a Blessed Solstice,
And a Happy New Year.

To the Future from Auld Lang Syne
(Traditional tune with words by Robert Burns)
Carolyn Lee Boyd

When Solstice rays shine on sacred wells
To bless the land Divine
We'll raise our song to Mighty Cailleach
From days of auld lang syne

From days of auld lang syne, my dears
From days of auld lang syne
We'll raise our song to Mighty Cailleach
From days of auld lang syne

Queen of Winter, Holy Hag
All Creation, Thine
Loving wisdom embraces all
Today and auld lang syne

Today and auld lang syne, my dears
Today and auld lang syne
Loving wisdom embraces all
Today and auld lang syne

From icy death rebirth must come
In flowers, birds, and kine*
Earth's promise from Her womb doth flow
To tomorrow from auld lang syne

To tomorrow from auld lang syne, my dears
To tomorrow from auld lang syne
Earth's promise from Her womb doth flow
To tomorrow from auld lang syne

So take my hand, my trusty fieres*

A new year's dawning fine
The Cailleach's here in joyful song
To the future from auld lang syne

To the future from auld lang syne, my dears
To the future from auld lang syne
We'll tak a cup o' kindness yet*
To the future from auld lang syne.

The Cailleach, envisioned usually as an old woman but sometimes as young, was known throughout Celtic realms as a Creatrix especially associated with the land and sacred wells, winter, storms, and regeneration in the spring.

*Glossary

Auld lang syne – olden times, times past (Scots)
Fiere – friend, companion (Scots)
Kine – cows (Old English)
Tak a cup o' kindness – raise a cup in friendship (Scots)

Athena
Kat Shaw

Alleluia! A Goddess is Born!
Laura Shannon

Woman, priestess, singer of praise: Greetings to you!

It is I, Athena, speaking.

At this time of year, we honour the dark and sing to bring the return of the light. Did you know that I, too, am a Goddess of death and rebirth? Like my Mesopotamian sister Inanna, I also went through an underworld journey.[27] In my case, I was still inside my mother's womb when I was swallowed – by my father, Zeus! But I survived, for I was stronger.

Today I will tell you the whole story. But first, let me remind you who I am.

I am Athena, Goddess of wisdom, source of protection, Goddess of peace. Within my domain are spinning and weaving, craft and skill, the creation of things both beautiful and useful. I brought the flute, the plow, the bridle, the chariot, and the olive tree with its wealth of food, healing, light, shade and wood for useful tools. Through reading and writing, I preserve precious knowledge. I protect the polis, not just the cities, but civilisation and culture born of women's craft and skill.

I have been honoured for thousands of years. My earliest aspects were serpent and bird, dwellers in realms above and below.[28] I am linked with bees and allied with water. I am the great cosmic Goddess of heaven and earth, and the sacred cycle of life, death and renewal.

As warrior goddess, I cannot be vanquished. Yet I am also the Goddess of peace. I teach strategy, diplomacy, defense; I guide

---

[27] Deacy 2008:20.
[28] Harrison 1908:306.

you to use your intelligence. I safeguard the sacred spaces: city and castle, acropolis, temple, house and harbour. As Goddess of justice, I teach right action, the time to move forward and the time to hold back. I protect all who come under my wing, with a heart of compassion for those who need healing.[29]

Logic and reason are my gifts: I am she who protects the mind. With my fierce flashing eyes, I see what is hidden, like my companion, the little owl, who bears my name: *Athene noctua*. I have been honoured with many names: Clear-Seeing, Great-Hearted, She Who Saves; Bright-Eyed, Untiring, the Healer, the Wise; the Guardian of the Temple, and simply, the Goddess. I am also Protector in Childbirth, as I protect all creative skills, and everything women bring into the world.

Still, you may have heard some slander – that I had no mother, that I side with the male. Don't believe those egregious lies! They are silly words of upstart playwrights, who have no power over me.[30] The enemies of women's wisdom are not the ones who should define us. So, pay no heed to all who talk, and remember who I truly am.

Now I'll tell how I was born. Of course, of course I had a mother! I am the daughter of Earth Goddess Metis, a clever shape-shifter whose very name means 'cunning' and 'counsel'. She was the wisest among all the mortals and all the gods.[31]

Zeus was my father, and they fell in love. It was Metis' wish to be pregnant with me, but Gaia and Ouranos, Zeus' grandparents, foresaw that the child would be wiser than he. Zeus was afraid when this prophecy came, so he tried to stop me being born. (Exactly as his father tried to do! Kronos swallowed his own children, until finally Zeus's mother, Rhea, tricked him with a swaddled stone, which he duly swallowed while she hid the baby. Rhea then raised Zeus in safety, nursed by the she-goat Amalthea,

---

[29] Shannon 2017:213-8.
[30] Aeschylus, *Eumenides* 736-8; Euripides, *Trojan Women*, 65-93.
[31] Hesiod, *Theogony* 886.

hidden on Crete in a mountain cave. You all know the story. But really – what fools! What is wrong with these fathers? Do they not understand the whole point of children? When a child excels its parents in strength and virtue, grace and wisdom, it's the sweetest gift and the truest tribute to the worth of the ancestral line.)

My mother Metis was divine, also immortal. She could not be killed. Zeus must have known this; still, there was a battle. To try to escape him, shape-shifting Metis changed her form into that of a fly, but Zeus opened his mouth and swallowed her up! Still pregnant with me! And my now-tiny mother, inside his head, went into labour. The birth pains began.

This gave Zeus an epic headache. Though he was a god, he could not stand the pain. As his agony grew, he pleaded for mercy, until finally Hephaestus came, the blacksmith god, with his mighty ax. And he split Zeus' skull wide open, and I was born! I could not be stopped. This is the story so often mistold. Yes, I sprang out of Zeus' head – fully grown, with a trilling cry – but before I emerged from my father's head, of course I emerged from my mother's womb. How else could it be? And so I was born. The insecure father, weak and jealous, could not stop me, for I was stronger. The prophecy came true.

Therefore I, the Goddess Athena, embody the wisdom which can't be destroyed. Even Zeus could not suppress my power, nor could he prevent my worship. People honoured us side by side for thousands of years in the ancient world, and over Athens I reigned alone. And when I leapt out, with the trilling cry? This was my birth song![32] Ulululí!

You've surely heard it. There is no other sound like this ancient cry, the women's joyful noise of praise. To make this powerful, piercing call, we raise our voices and flutter our tongues. At births and weddings, when guests arrive, as a shout of triumph, when there is news: we raise the rafters, we shake the sky. This ear-splitting call of jubilation, which you may know as ululation, was

---

[32] Pindar, Olympian Ode 7.35.

always part of praise and prayer; the women of Athens made this cry when they called on me for their protection.[33]

In the Horn of Africa, it's called ilil.[34] Its Sanskrit root is ululí, an 'outcry of prosperity'.[35] The ancient Greek is ὀλολυγή/ologugê, 'to cry aloud'.[36] Latin ululare gives us ululation. And Gaelic uileliugh is a 'wail of lamentation'.[37] All these words sound like the cry itself – and that's how you know how my voice sounded, when I cried out when I was born. In Hebrew, the root is hillel – 'to trill', but also 'to praise', with the plural command hallalu, plus 'yah' for Yahweh, the name of God, giving Hallalu-yah, Praise ye God![38] And Hallelujah, in Greek and Latin, becomes the word you have grown up singing: Alleluia, Alleluia.[39]

So, in this Solstice season, as you sing these hymns, you'll be singing my birth cry, over and over. Alleluia is a mantra: it's a sacred word of power and cannot truly be translated. It praises God, it praises Goddess, it commands us all to praise. And it's the earth-shaking joyful cry which announces the birth of the Great Goddess. Remember me and sing my name. And whenever you sing Alleluia, let my strength and power, my peace and wisdom, and my spirit of survival, be born triumphantly anew in you. No power can vanquish women's wisdom, nor can it be hidden any longer. We birth it ourselves with a cry of joy.

Alleluia, Hallelujah! Ulululululí!!

---

[33] Rigoglioso 2010:61.
[34] Buxton 1970:65.
[35] Jacobs 2008:27-28.
[36] Rigoglioso 2010:60.
[37] https://www.etymonline.com/word/ululation
[38] https://www.etymonline.com/word/hallelujah
[39] https://en.wikipedia.org/wiki/Hallelujah

References

Aeschylus. Translated by Smyth, Herbert Weir. Loeb Classical Library Volumes 145 & 146. Cambridge, MA. Harvard University Press. 1926.

Buxton, D. 1970. *The Abyssinians*. New York: Praeger.

Deacy, S. 2008. *Athena*. London and New York: Routledge.

Euripides. 1891. *The Plays of Euripides*, translated by E. P. Coleridge, Vol I. London: George Bell and Sons.

Harrison, Jane Ellen. 1903. *Prolegomena to the Study of Greek Religion*. Cambridge: Cambridge University Press.

Hesiod. 2007. *Works Of Hesiod And The Homeric Hymns*. Translated by Hine, D. Chicago: University of Chicago Press.

Jacobs, J. 2008. 'Ululation in Levantine society: The cultural reproduction of an affective vocalization'. PhD dissertation. https://repository.upenn.edu/dissertations/AAI3309571

Online Etymology Dictionary, accessed March 13, 2022.

Pindar. 1990. *Odes*. Translated by Diane Arnson Svarlien.

Rigoglioso, M. (2010). *Virgin Mother Goddesses of Antiquity*. New York: Palgrave Macmillan.

Shannon, L. (2017). 'Medusa and Athena: Ancient Allies in Healing Women's Trauma' in *Re-Visioning Medusa: from Monster to Divine Wisdom*. Edited by G. Livingstone, T. Hendren and P. Daly. Girl God Books, 2017, 206-222.

Astraea
Kat Shaw

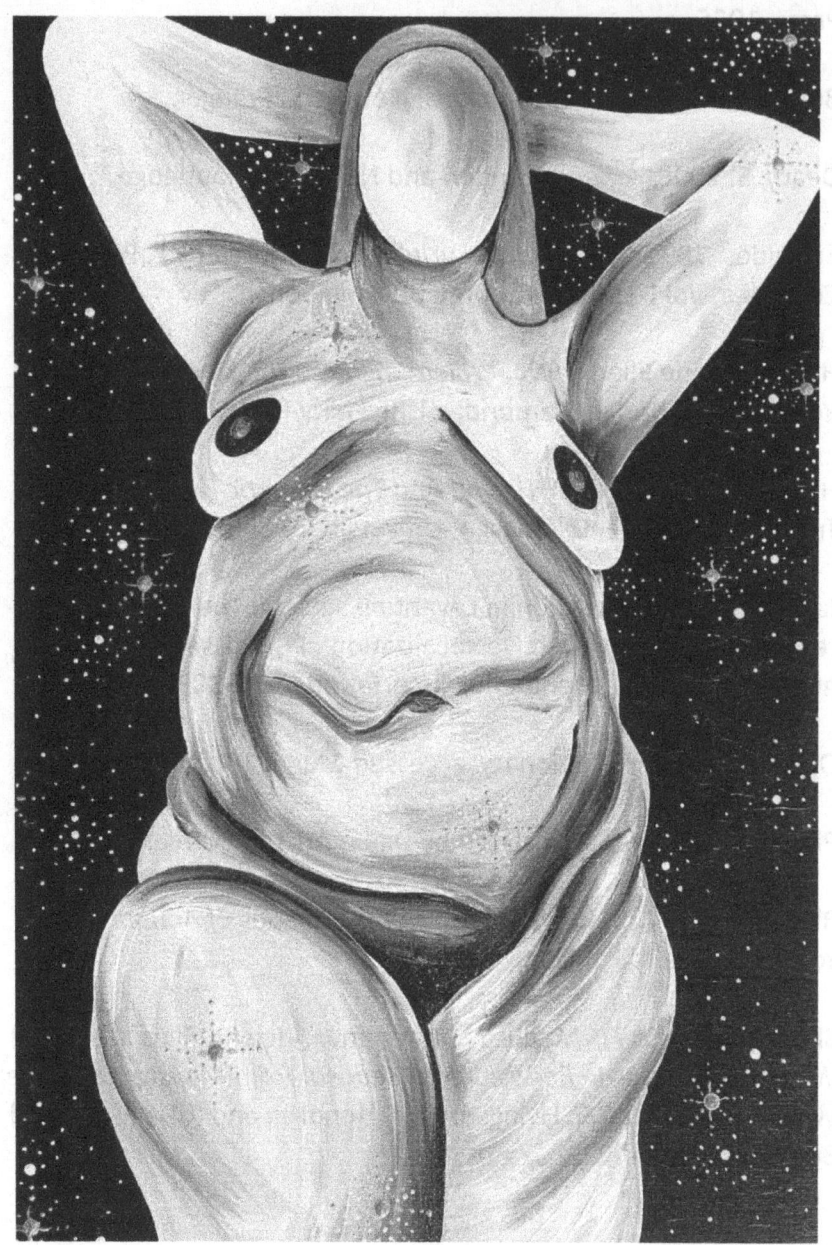

Hallelujah Chorus
Trista Hendren and Anders Løberg

Hallelujah! Hallelujah! Hallelujah! Hallelujah! Hallelujah!
Hallelujah! Hallelujah! Hallelujah! Hallelujah! Hallelujah!
For the Goddess Benevolent reigneth
Hallelujah! Hallelujah! Hallelujah! Hallelujah!

For the Goddess Benevolent reigneth
Hallelujah! Hallelujah! Hallelujah! Hallelujah!

For the Goddess Benevolent reigneth
Hallelujah! Hallelujah! Hallelujah! Hallelujah! Hallelujah!
Hallelujah! Hallelujah! Hallelujah! Hallelujah! Hallelujah!
Hallelujah! Hallelujah! Hallelujah! Hallelujah! Hallelujah!

The Queendom of this world
Is become the Queendom of our hearts
And of Her love, and of Her love

And She shall reign for ever and ever
And She shall reign for ever and ever
And She shall reign for ever and ever
And She shall reign forever and ever

Queen of Queens (Forever and ever Hallelujah! Hallelujah!)
And Mom of moms (Forever and ever Hallelujah! Hallelujah!)
Queen of Queens (Forever and ever Hallelujah! Hallelujah!)
And Mom of moms (Forever and ever Hallelujah! Hallelujah!)
Queen of Queens (Forever and ever Hallelujah! Hallelujah!)
And Mom of moms (Queen of Queens and Mom of moms)

And She shall reign (And She shall reign)
And She shall reign
And She shall reign forever and ever

Queen of Queens (Forever and ever)
And Mom of Moms (Hallelujah! Hallelujah!)

And She shall reign forever and ever

Queen of Queens! and Mom of moms!
Queen of Queens! and Mom of moms!
And She shall reign forever and ever

Forever and ever (Queen of Queens!)
Forever and ever (Mom of Moms!)
Hallelujah! Hallelujah!
Hallelujah! Hallelujah!
Hallelujah!

Note from Trista: This is a difficult song with many parts. I still have to work up to singing the Soprano part I grew up with weeks into December since I don't usually sing this high anymore. If you don't know this song well, I suggest singing along to the Mormon Tabernacle Choir on YouTube for now—and jumping in when you can. I have sung it with them so many times that I now hear the SHE very distinctly! It always brings tears to my eyes.

Blessed Solstice
Trista Hendren

Many people wondered why we took the time to re-write these old Christmas Carols. The attitude seemed to be, *Just Move On!* Some were even disgusted and retorted—*Write your own songs!*

It's not that simple. These songs were imprinted upon us from an early age. As Mary Daly noted, we were bombarded with them.[40] In fact, we still are—year after year! For me to finalize my divorce from Christianity, I needed a replacement. As Carol P. Christ wrote:

> "Even people who no longer 'believe in God' or participate in the institutional structure of patriarchal religion still may not be free of the power of the symbolism of God the Father. A symbol's effect does not depend on rational assent, for a symbol also functions on levels of the psyche other than the rational. Symbol systems cannot simply be rejected; they must be replaced. Where there is no replacement, the mind will revert to familiar structures at times of crisis, bafflement, or defeat."[41]

The fact is, that I love singing these songs—despite how toxic I now find many of the words.

I grew up singing the Hallelujah Chorus every year in choirs at both church and school. My daughter will do no such thing. I would never impose those words on her. I can still fully feel their impact on me as a subservient daughter of Patriarchy.

---

[40] Daly, Mary. *Gyn/Ecology: The Metaethics of Radical Feminism*. Beacon Press, 1990.

[41] Christ, Carol P. "Why Women Need the Goddess" from the "Keynote Address at the "Great Goddess Re-emerging" Conference at the University of Santa Cruz in the spring of 1978 and reprinted in *Womanspirit Rising: A Feminist Reader on Religion* by Carol P. Christ and Judith Plaskow.

I want all our daughters to know their innate sovereignty. The symbol of the Goddess lights a path to truth. Carol P. Christ wrote:

> "The simplest and most basic meaning of the symbol of the Goddess is the acknowledgment of the legitimacy of female power as a beneficent and independent power."[42]

My dream is that choirs around the world will sing the re-written carols with a finale of the Hallelujah Chorus. We hope these songs bring deep meaning to your holiday season—and deep peace to the world at large.

All of us at Girl God Books wish you a VERY Merry and Blessed Solstice—and a Happy New Year!

---

[42] Christ, Carol P. "Why Women Need the Goddess," 1978.

Blessed Be!
Andrea Redmond

List of Contributors

Alissa DeLaFuente lives and works in the Pacific Northwest. Her fiction, nonfiction, and poetry have appeared in scientific and literary journals, including *Gold Man Review, Red Savina Review,* and others. In response to the pandemic, she wrote and self-published a book on time management and gentle goal-setting to help young people manage the chaos. It came out in May 2020, and is titled *Get Your Life Together: A practical guide to getting organized.* She regularly serves as a prose judge for the International Latino Book Awards. Visit her website at www.alissadelafuente.com to learn more.

Anders Løberg has worked with the environment for most of his career. He has recently returned to his passion for bikes full-time at Kirkens Bymisjon Pedalen sykkelverksted in Bergen. He has been car-free for nearly 20 years as a firm believer in Human Power Transport. Anders gets nearly everywhere on bike or foot – including hauling over 2000 kilos of cement for the Goddess of Willendorf Statue in Bergen. He has run Velomobile Media for 15 years. https://www.velomobil.no

Anders has been instrumental at Girl God Books since the beginning, encouraging Trista to publish The Girl God. He manages the website, creates videos and book covers, and much more! This is his first written contribution to Girl God Books.

Anders enjoys fiddling, singing, eating, and home repair projects.

Andrea Redmond has been a feminist rights activist, artist and pagan for over 50 years. She has been a devotee of The Morrigan since a young girl.

She was born on Prince Edward Island, Canada of Irish descent. She moved to Ireland with her young family and there, she was one of the first women in Belfast to paint wall murals. Her first mural in 1983 honoured women's rights activists from Ireland and South Africa. She has painted over 40 murals with similar themes and her work has been featured in a number of publications and films on Northern Ireland.

She has worked and chaired a number of women's, art and multicultural groups. She has taught programs in art, community development and youth work. She is a mother to three children and returned to education in her 40s, completing her PhD, at the University of Ulster.

Andrea currently resides in rural Donegal, Ireland where she operates her art studio/workshop. Her artwork is in permanent collections and galleries in Ireland, Canada and the United States.

Anique Radiant Heart is High Priestess of the Global Goddess, Goddess Scholar, Sacred Singer Songwriter, author of *Chanting the Chakras – A Way to the Goddess Through Energetic Use of Voice* and *The 33 Teachings of Kuan Yin*. She is an internationally acclaimed Spiritual Teacher. Anique Radiant Heart is a well-loved member of the International Goddess Community.

Anique has created CDs of original music celebrating the Goddess, produced Goddess festivals, conferences, and led tours to sacred sites all over the world. In 2007, she was crowned a Foremother of the Australian Goddess Community at the Australian Goddess Conference. In 2010, she manifested the Temple of the Global Goddess for all to enjoy, and began teaching a 3-year Priestess Training program in the Temple of the Global Goddess in Maitland. Today, there are 2 Temples of the Global Goddess – the Mother House in Maitland and the Sister House in Sydney. She now has a dedicated grove of ordained Priestesses with another round of training which began in 2017. Anique has organized Goddess Conferences and Festivals in Australia since 1996, and for the past 4 years has been the co-visionary with respected Aboriginal Elder Bilawara Lee of the Australian Goddess Conference – the first conference ever in Australia to be held by an Aboriginal and Non-Aboriginal sister.

In 2017, at the Glastonbury Goddess Conference, Anique revealed and launched her Vision for an International Priestess Convocation in Crete in 2020. This gathering is designed to put into place strategies to bring about the unfolding of The Motherworld – a platform for social, political and spiritual change in the world. Dedicated to assisting women to reclaim their natural spiritual authority, Anique continues to teach women the power and joy that comes from a sacred path which celebrates the Divine Feminine. For the last 25 years, she has travelled for 3 months each year to share her teachings and music with daughters and sons of the Goddess all over the world.

http://goddess.net.au/

Barbara O'Meara is a published writer, co-editor of *Soul Seers Irish Anthology of Celtic Shamanism*, and a professional visual artist. She has recently illustrated *My Name is Brigid* by Jessica Johnson, published by Girl God Books.

Exhibitions include 'B.O.R.N. -Babies of Ravaged Nations', group shows Lockhart Gallery New York & 'The Drawing Box' Europe, America, Far East & 'Herstory' Brigids of the World & Black Lives Matter.

Community projects i.e., 'Stitched With Love' Tuam Baby Blanket laid over the burial site at the Mother & Child Home, shown at KOLO International Women's Non Killing Cross Borders Summit in Sarajevo held by Bosnian women survivors. She is continually developing empowering women's 'Art as Activism' events i.e., 'Sort Our Smears' Campaign at 'Festival of Feminisms'.

Her Collections include: *Microsoft, ESB, Dept Foreign Affairs, Irish Life, Impact Trade Union, Bologna District Council, Behaviour & Attitudes.*

A recent art review stated: "Barbara O'Meara's recent paintings dealing with home and Covid are extremely beautiful and extremely coherent in their communication. Rarely is it seen where painting is used to convey complex emotional human conditions." www.barbaraomearaartist.com

Carol P. Christ (1945-2021) died peacefully on July 14th, 2021 from cancer. Carol was and will remain one of the foremothers and most brilliant voices of the Women's Spirituality movement. At the conference on "The Great Goddess Re-Emerging" at the University of California at Santa Cruz in the spring of 1978, Carol delivered the keynote address, "Why Women Need the Goddess: Phenomenological, Psychological, and Political Reflections." Christ proposed four compelling reasons why women might turn to the Goddess: the affirmation and legitimation of female power as beneficent; affirmation of the female body and its life cycles; affirmation of women's will; and affirmation of women's bonds with one another and their positive female heritage (Christ 1979).

Carol graduated from Yale University with a PhD in Religious Studies and went on to teach as a feminist scholar of women and religion, women's spirituality, and Goddess studies, at institutions including Columbia University, Harvard Divinity School, Pomona College, San Jose State University, and the California Institute of Integral Studies, where she was an adjunct professor since the inception of the Women's Spirituality, Philosophy and Religion graduate studies program in 1993. Christ published eight profoundly thoughtful and inspiring books, several in collaboration with her friend and colleague Judith Plaskow, whom she met at Yale:

- *Diving Deep and Surfacing: Women Writers on Spiritual Quest* (1986)
- *Woman Spirit Rising: A Feminist Reader in Religion,* an anthology co-edited with Judith Plaskow (1992)
- *Odyssey with the Goddess: A Spiritual Quest in Crete* (1995)
- *Weaving the Visions: New Patterns in Feminist Spirituality.* Anthology co-edited with Judith Plaskow (1989)
- *Laughter of Aphrodite: Reflections on a Journey to the Goddess* (1987)

- *Rebirth of the Goddess: Finding Meaning in Feminist Spirituality* (1998)
- *She Who Changes: Re-imaging the Divine in the World* (2004)
- *Goddess and God in the World: Conversations in Embodied Theology*. Co-authored with Judith Plaskow (2016)

Christ's first book, about women writers on spiritual quest, is a book of spiritual feminist literary criticism that focused on feminist authors Kate Chopin, Margaret Atwood, Doris Lessing, Adriene Rich, and Ntozake Shange. She discovers four key aspects to women's spiritual quest: the experience of nothingness; awakening (to the powers that are greater than oneself, often found in nature); insight (into the meaning of one's life); and a new naming (in one's own terms). She emphasizes the importance of telling women's stories in order to move beyond the stories told about women by the male-centered patriarchy. Her concluding chapter speaks of a "Culture of Wholeness," that encompasses women's quest for wholeness, and she adds that, for this wholeness to be realized, the personal spiritual quest needs to be combined with the quest for social justice.

After first travelling to Greece in 1981 with the Aegean Women's Studies Institute led by her friend Ellen Boneparth, Carol fell in love with the country. She chose to live in Greece, first in Molivos on the beautiful island of Lesbos, and then moving recently to Heraklion, Crete. She had a passion for saving the environment and was active in the Green movement in Greece. she also had a love for swimming in the Aegean Sea and sharing Greek food and wine with friends in Greece and from overseas.

Carol's fascination with Crete, ancient and modern, led her to found the Ariadne Institute for the Study of Myth and Ritual, through which she offered an educational tour, "Pilgrimage to the Goddess" twice annually. These tours introduced many to a direct experience of the ancient Earth Mother Goddess in Crete (goddessariadne.org).

In her most recent article, for the *Encyclopedia of Women in World Religion: Faith and Culture*, Christ wrote about the Goddess religion and culture of her beloved island of Crete, and the roles women played in that "egalitarian matriarchal" civilization. Her eloquent words speak not only to the Goddess religion of ancient Crete, but also to the spirituality and ethical values she also cherished, which are much needed in our own culture today.

> "As discerners and guardians of the mysteries, women created rituals to celebrate the Source of Life and to pass the secrets of agriculture, pottery, and weaving down through the generations. The major rituals of the agricultural cycle involved blessing the seeds before planting, offering the first fruits of the harvest to the Goddess, and sharing the bounty of the harvest in communal feasts. These rituals establish that life is a gift of the Goddess and institute gift-giving as a cultural practice. As women controlled the secrets of agriculture, it makes sense that land was held by maternal clans, that kinship and inheritance passed through the maternal line, and that governance and decision-making for the group were in the hands of the elders of the maternal clan. In this context, the intelligence, love, and generosity of mothers and clan mothers would have been understood to reflect the intelligence, love, and generosity of the Goddess."[43]

Carol's Obituary was written by **Mara Lynn Keller, PhD** and **Ellen Boneparth**, who encouraged sharing. We thank them for this beautiful tribute to her memory.

Carolyn Lee Boyd is a writer, student drummer, and herb and native plant gardener. Her essays, short stories, memoirs, reviews, and poetry have been published in, among others, *Feminism and Religion, Return to Mago E-Magazine, Sagewoman, The Goddess Pages, Matrifocus*, and *The Beltane Papers*, and various

---

[43] Carol P. Christ, "Crete, Religion and Culture" Encyclopedia of *Women in World Religions: Faith and Culture across History* [2 volumes] edited by Susan de-Gaia | Nov 16, 2018 ABC-Clio Santa Barbara 2019.

anthologies. She would love for you to visit her at her website, www.goddessinateapot.com where you can find some of her free e-books to download.

Chelsea Arrington was born in a town named after a poet, and so The Norns decreed she was fated to become a poet as well. Her work can be found in the magazines, *Spectral Realms, The Audient Void, Eternal Haunted Summer*, the folk horror anthology, *A Walk in a Darker Wood* and elsewhere. Chelsea is a practicing witch in an active coven. She hoards books, movies, and art and lives in the Greater Los Angeles area with her Viking and their children.

Cheryl Braganza (February 25, 1945 – December 16, 2016) was a gifted artist and poet. Of Goan origin, she was born in Bombay and grew up in Lahore where her parents owned Braganza Hotel (referenced in "Freedom at Midnight" Collins & Lapierre). After studying languages and the arts in Rome and classical piano in London, she moved to Montreal in 1966. Essentially self-taught, her subjects vary from evocative landscapes, lush florals to vibrant figures of Indian women.

She exhibited regularly and established herself as a Quebec artist with a style of her own, using brilliant color and texture to express emotion. You can see more of her work at cherylbraganza.com. Her work is shared with the permission of her beloved son, Miguel, who cared for her the last 13 years of her life.

*Cheryl's Story – written by her son, Miguel Da Costa Frias

Some people leave such a ripple on the wave of humanity, that it floats us all toward one another. This was my mother.

A musician with raw unbridled talent, Cheryl was offered a scholarship to Juilliard when she was sixteen. From a young age, she played the piano, the organ, the accordion, and the harmonica with equal versatility. She began to paint in her 20's and discovered that she was a gifted painter.

She was diagnosed with a bone-related cancer on her 60th birthday in 2005 and came a hairsbreadth from death four times, only to fight her way back to life each time. For the last decade, while fighting cancer, a handwritten quote from Goethe rested on top of her easel: "Rest not. Life is sweeping by; go and dare before you die. Something mighty and sublime, leave behind to conquer time." Little did we know how much she would take this quote to heart or put it into action.

Cheryl developed her painting talent with exponential speed. When asked why she was working so feverishly, she answered "I'm in a race against time. I have so much to say and so much more to bring into the world…" In her last five years of life, she produced more artwork and published more writing than she produced in the previous 20 years.

In 2008, she was named Montreal's Woman of the Year for using her art as a tool to fight for women's rights all over the world. She was featured in hundreds of media worldwide and was then elected President of the prestigious Women's Art Society of Montreal, which she grew dramatically.

Her effect on people became evident in the thousands of emails she received from people she inspired across the world.

She lived longer than anyone in recorded history with myeloma cancer in the brain, refusing painkillers because she didn't want her senses affected. Her only desire was to experience every moment in living color until her very last breath. Following her last remission, limping in pain, she decided to learn jazz from scratch, started her own jazz band and played to sold out crowds in Griffintown for two years.

Our mother believed that in order to enjoy true happiness, she should live each moment as if it were her last. Yesterday will never return. Tomorrow may never happen. While we may speak of the past or of the future, the only reality we have is that of right now, the present instant.

Confronting the reality of death enabled her to blossom with unlimited creativity, courage and joy. The more broken her body became over the years, the more she painted soaring images of birds, and butterflies, and dancing women.

She was never alone, surrounded by an ever-increasing group of family and friends who grew to love her (and each other). When the cancer finally paralyzed her body, it was our turn to bring the joy to her; kidnapping her from the hospital for secret outings, regaling her with live music every day for nine months. And even then, we marveled how she could still paint magical tapestries of colour and love with her face, her voice and her mind.

She died peacefully in her sleep after seeing her three children; her soul soaring to the beautiful places reflected in her art.

Claire Dorey
Goldsmiths: BA Hons Fine Art.
Main Employment: Journalist and Creative, UK and overseas.
Artist: Most notable group show: *Pillow Talk* at the Tate Modern. Included in the *Pillow Talk Book*.

Curator: 3 x grass roots SLWA exhibitions and educational events on the subject of Female Empowerment, showcasing female artists, academic speeches and local musicians. Silence Is Over – Raising awareness on violence towards women; Ex Voto – Existential Mexican Art Therapy; Heo – Female empowerment in the self-portrait.

Extra study: Suppressed Female History: History of the Goddess; Accessing Creative Wisdom; Sound and Breath Work; Reiki Master; Colour Therapy; Hand Mudras; Reflexology; Sculpture.

Teaching Workshops: Sculpture and Drawing.

Connie Barlow, Ypsilanti, Michigan USA.

Dale Allen is a veteran of corporate, creative, and commercial communications. Her extensive resume includes hundreds of voice-over, on-camera, theater and live presentation projects. Dale was honored to twice present to the United Nations Commission on the Status of Women, her one-woman show, *In Our Right Minds*™, Guiding Women to Their Strength as Leaders, Leading Men to Strength Without Armor. Her encore was requested by the Vice President of the Commission, Ambassador

Carlos Enrique Garcia Gonzales. In October 2021, she presented her new film version of the piece to the Parliament of the World's Religions. She has brought her talents to scores of audiences - across the U.S., into Canada, and from Kauai to Dubai. Described as having the energy of "a Cape Canaveral lift-off," she thoroughly engages and inspires her audience, which ranges from highly educated corporate leaders to teenage girls seeking their place in the world.

Deborah A. Meyerriecks is a self-dedicated Witch, Community Priestess, and a retired NYC Medic. Originally from New York City, she currently lives in the liminal space of the Colorado River Valley in the Mohave Desert of N.W. Arizona. Growing up in the Catholic Church of her mother, Deborah was volun-told into service as a choir member and leader of song, often re-imagining the lyrics of the hymns to fit her magick and devotional practices. Her first book, *Macha and the Medic: Service and Priesthood on the Frontlines of Life* was released Spring 2022. Her new favorite title that was bestowed on her by her community is 'Spiritual EMT.' Deborah is a Shadow Care Facilitator who enjoys traveling, sharing what she knows and learning more about herself and her craft though teaching. Contact her at WillowMoon@yahoo.com or www.WillowMoonConsulting.com to see what she's currently offering.

Glenys Livingstone, Ph.D. has been on a Goddess path since 1979. She is the author of *PaGaian Cosmology: Re-inventing Earth-based Goddess Religion*, which fuses the indigenous traditions of Old Europe with scientific theory, feminism and a poetic relationship with place. She lives in the Blue Mountains of Australia where she has facilitated Seasonal ceremony, taught classes, and mentored apprentices. In 2014, Glenys co-facilitated the Mago Pilgrimage to Korea with Dr. Helen Hwang. Glenys is a contributor to Goddesses in World Culture edited by Patricia Monaghan (2011), and to *Foremothers of the Women's Spirituality Movement* edited by Miriam Robbins Dexter and Vicki Noble (2015). She recently produced *PaGaian Cosmology Meditations* CDs, and teaches a year-long on-line course "Celebrating Cosmogenesis in the Wheel of the Year." Her book and CDs are available at her website http://pagaian.org

Hallie Iglehart Austen grew up on a farm and has lived close to the earth for most of her life. Her lifelong interest in goddesses began at the age of twelve when she started studying ancient Greek language and mythology at Bryn Mawr School. After graduating from Brown University, she drove from England to Nepal and back again over the course of a year. This journey, described in her book, *Womanspirit:A Guide to Women's Wisdom*, led to her synthesis of spirituality and feminism, which she first started teaching in 1974. She has led workshops, rituals and conferences at the University of California, United Nations International Women's Conference, and Graduate Theological Union among others. She created *Womanspirit Meditations* and collected worldwide Goddess art, myth and meditations in her book, The Heart of the Goddess: Art, Myth and Meditations of the World's Sacred Feminine. To view video with music from the book, see https://heartgoddess.net.

In 2001, driven by her love of marine life, she found another way of serving the Mother and co-*founded Seaflow: Protect Our Living Oceans* to educate people about the dangers of active sonars and other ocean noise to whales, dolphins and all sea life. Hallie continued her passion for sustainable living by building two model green homes, one in bamboo. In 2010, she founded *All One Ocean* to educate people about the danger of ocean plastic pollution and offer action tools.

Presently, Hallie fundraises for indigenous/climate causes, Black urban farms and democracy. Hallie uses Austen as her last name, to honor her matrilineal heritage. She lives in the San Francisco Bay Area, and offers private consultations and classes.

Jassy Watson is a contemporary Australian artist living on the glorious sub-tropical Queensland coast. You will find her working full-time from her garden studio and beachside gallery set among the sugar cane fields, red dirt and coral coastline of the Bundaberg region. While formally trained in the arts in her early years, a life of experimenting and exploring led Jassy to develop a unique way of working with images that feel genuine. She works primarily in acrylics and mixed media but has more recently returned to oils as her preferred medium. Her use of materials is bold and assertive, especially evident in her use of heavy black inky lines, and a palette as vibrant as nature itself.

Jassy's paintings are largely inspired by scenes of the everyday that she records as part of her daily drawing practice. From the lounge to the ever-changing landscape of her region to tropical Bali and even her own backyard, her larger than life paintings are captivating, at times sentimental, while contrastingly quirky in perspective. With an intentional, intuitive and confident approach, Jassy's deep connection to land and place truly shines through in these unique interpretations of the world around her.

Her work hangs in private and public collections and has been selected and exhibited in numerous solo, group and award shows at leading galleries, with her most recent solo *The Sacred and Mundane; Scenes of the Everyday* exhibited by Hervey Bay Regional Art Gallery. Further, her paintings have also been featured in a number of international online and in-text publications, including journals, blogs, university textbooks, published books and other texts. Most recently, her work has appeared in the Summer edition of Australia's *National Art/Edit* magazine. While most of her work is done at the canvas, Jassy is also very passionate about sharing her artistic skill and wisdom with others. As a certified Intentional Creativity® teacher she has been teaching from her home studio and travelling the globe offering educational programs and retreats for the past 8 years.

For more information, go to Jassy.com.au

Kat Shaw prides herself on breaking through the stereotypical views of beauty that have been cast upon society by the media, having made her name painting the glorious reality that is a woman's body.

Her nude studies of real women garnered unprecedented popularity within only a few short months, as women were crying out for themselves to be portrayed in art, rather than the airbrushed images of the perfection of the female form that are so rife in today's culture.

After graduating with a fine art degree, Kat achieved a successful full-time teaching career for 14 years and continues to teach art part-time whilst passionately pursuing her mission of world domination by empowering as many women as possible to reach their fullest potential by embracing their bodies and loving themselves wholeheartedly.

Kat spreads her inspirational magic through her artwork, her Wellbeing business "Fabulously Imperfect," and her dedication to Goddess energy.

Reiki is a huge part of her life, and as a Reiki Master, Kat is committed to sharing Reiki, teaching Usui, Angelic and Karuna Reiki, and channelling Reiki energy through her artwork to uplift and heal.

As a Sister of Avalon, Kat also works directly with her Goddess consciousness, connecting to Goddess and Priestess energy and translating it into Divine Feminine infused paintings to inspire women and spread Goddess love.

Kat is also a belly dancer and an avid pioneer to improve the lives of rescue animals, and mum to a gorgeous teenage daughter.

Kay Louise Aldred (www.kaylouisealdred.com) is a researcher, writer and teacher, who catalyses individual, institutional and collective evolution – through education, embodiment and creativity – amalgamating metacognition, intuition and instinct. Her books include; *Mentorship with Goddess: Growing Sacred Womanhood*, published 2022, *Making Love with the Divine: Sacred, Ecstatic, Erotic, Experiences* and *Somatic Shamanism: Your Fleshy Knowing as the Tree of Life*, both scheduled for 2023.

Kay and her husband Dan Aldred, are co-authoring a book together, *Embodied Structure: Creating Safe Space for Learning, Facilitating and Sharing*, scheduled for 2023.

Laura Shannon is considered one of the 'grandmothers' of the worldwide Sacred/Circle Dance movement. For over thirty years she has been researching and teaching traditional Greek, Balkan, and Armenian women's circle dances, with a focus on their roots in the Goddess cultures of Neolithic Old Europe as articulated by Marija Gimbutas. She has university qualifications in Intercultural Studies, Dance Movement Therapy, and Myth, Cosmology and the Sacred, and is currently a PhD candidate in Dance and Religious Studies. Laura has been on the faculty of the Sacred Dance Department of the Findhorn Foundation since 1998 and is Founding Director of the German non-profit Athena Institute for Women's Dance and Culture. In 2021 Carol P. Christ chose Laura to be her successor as Director of the Ariadne Institute for the Study of Myth and Ritual and the Goddess Pilgrimage to Crete. Laura has published widely on women's sacred dance and writes a regular blog on feminismandreligion.com. More information at www.laurashannon.net or Laura's page on academia.edu.

Dr Lynne Sedgmore CBE is a Priestess of Avalon, Poetess, retired Chief Executive, soul coach and Non-executive board member. She lives in Glastonbury UK. She is founder, tutor and author of the *Goddess Luminary Leadership Wheel* trainings and book (Changemakers 2021). A unique combination of liberating leadership, feminism and Goddess spirituality offered through the Glastonbury Goddess Temple. She co-wrote the Avalon Anthem and her three poetry collections are *Enlivenment* (Chrysalis Press 2013), *Healing through the Goddess* (TheaSpeaks Press 2017) and *Crone* (TheaSpeaks Press 2019). She has 3 daughters and 2 granddaughters and loves singing hymns and carols. Her website link is https://www.lynnesedgmore.co.uk/

Margaret (Margi) Curtis (b. 1957) (Master of Creative Arts, Grad. Dip. Transpersonal Breathwork, Dip. LIS), witch, writer, artist, healer and activist, lives in Wollongong, NSW, with her family and a black cat. Published in magazines and anthologies, in print and online, including *Midnight Echo* and *Spectral Realms*, she is the author of four collections of poetry, including *Voice of the Goddess and other poems* (1991).

Mary Saracino is a novelist, memoir writer, and poet. Her most recent novel, *Heretics: A Love Story* (2014) was published by Pearlsong Press. Her novel, *The Singing of Swans* (Pearlsong Press 2006) was named a 2007 Lambda Literary Awards finalist in the Spirituality category. For more information about Mary and her work, visit www.marysaracino.com and http://www.pearlsong.com/mary_saracino.htm

Megha Morganfield now lives in Tucson Arizona, USA. But in 1983, she was living in Carbondale, Illinois and attending Southern Illinois University. For a wellness course in her masters degree program, she was reading Mary Daly's *Gyn/Ecology*.

Megha had been singing and writing music since her teens. It was November and Christmas caroling was around the corner, in terms of time. A quiet afternoon of reading changed her life and that of many others who only knew the traditional carols before.

As she read Mary Daly's words, her perspective was completely changed. Daly wrote: "The Christmas carols had become subliminal messages piped into the department stores by the patriarchy, to say it is the only game in town." Megha literally burst into tears, and after sitting stunned for some time, she resolved to reclaim the carols for the Goddess.

In a writing fit one afternoon, she rewrote 13 carols and realigned them with what she believed would've been their original intent... to celebrate the light, our earth mother, the elements, peace and love. The tunes, the "traditional" tunes, more ancient certainly than the Christian religion, now sung the glory of the faith in the eternal cycles.

From there, Megha turned her life to music, full time. Her music, often accompanied by her celtic harp, includes Megha Morganfield's *Winter Solstice Carols* – which along with her other six CDs can be found on cdbaby.com, Spotify, Amazon, and in the hands of singers all over the globe. And thus, the children who have learned the Solstice Carols now hear "Oh Rest Ye Merry Folks and Friends, Let nothing you dismay… there's so much to be joyful for in nature's great display…" everywhere the music plays.

Pat Daly (editor) is a mother of three daughters and proud grandma. A published author / writer on career and job search issues, Pat lives in Portland, Oregon.

Rebekah Myers is dedicated to opening doors of understanding on behalf of women everywhere. She is the founder/facilitator of Sacred Sisters Full Moon Circle, which serves as a virtual Facebook and Instagram public page, a private Facebook group for women, and an actual women's circle that meets in-person. For International Women's Day in March of 2018, Rebekah was honored to have been one of five women recognized by KSL as Utah's most inspirational women.

Through her social anthropologist parents, Rebekah spent memorable time with the Iroquois (a matrilineal people) of Six Nations Reserve in Ontario, Canada. This experience significantly informed her life for the good. Rebekah has had a life-long interest in and passion for folklore, mythology, and ancient history, and has spent significant time in these worlds. Although Rebekah formally came later in life to women's spirituality, she has found such fulfillment on this path, that there is no turning back. As a writer, teacher, director, award-winning singer/performer/actress, mother, grandmother, and wedding officiator, Rebekah works to empower, enlighten, and uplift women and their brothers. She knows it is possible to heal the wounds of patriarchy and live with depth, meaning, and joy.

Sara Star paints Goddesses, magic, altars and the wonder of nature from her home in Oregon. She lives with her husband and their cats. She can be found online at Spiritscraft.com and SaraStar.com.

Sharon Smith is a writer, ghost writer, editor, and proofreader with a passion for helping women reconnect with their Authentic Selves and Voices. She loves and honors the Great Mother in all Her many forms, and has a deep connection to Nature. She identifies as a Green Witch and follows an eclectic spiritual path that is a blending of Native American and Celtic Teachings, both in her ancestral line.

Painting is **Sue Ellen Parkinson**'s doorway through to understanding the world. Creativity is her form of prayer. When she paints a person, she is honoring that Being. That experience is one of deep connection that brings her into wholeness. That's as important to her as oxygen. Her focus is largely about re-visioning, and celebrating womankind—lifting them up. Exploring the Christian mystics has produced a profound change in her. She has found herself particularly drawn to Mary Magdalene. For her, Magdalene is the archetype who represents All Women who have been inaccurately portrayed in history. It's been a healing experience to restore her identity, and the identity of other great women, to the wise and sovereign beings that she believes they are. In so doing, she has become more empowered herself. www.sueellenparkinson.com

Trista Hendren founded Girl God Books in 2011 to support a necessary unraveling of the patriarchal world view of divinity. Her first book—*The Girl God*, a children's picture book—was a response to her own daughter's inability to see herself reflected in God. Since then, she has published more than 45 books by a dozen women from across the globe with help from her family and friends. She lives in Bergen, Norway. You can learn more about her projects at www.thegirlgod.com.

Trista's Acknowledgments

I would like to acknowledge my co-editors. My mother, **Pat Daly**, has edited each and every one of my books. There would be no Girl God Books without her many contributions. I was thrilled to also work with my dear Sister **Sharon Smith** on this project—who shares my passion for dismantling all things patriarchal. I love you Sis!

Tremendous gratitude to **Kat Shaw** for allowing us to feature her gorgeous painting as the cover art—and for sharing the story of Goddess Berchta. I love you my Rainbow Goddess twin!

Special thanks to **Miriam Robbins Dexter** for giving detailed feedback on the early copy of the book. I love you to the moon— and am tremendously grateful for the love, feedback, and support you have shown me over the years.

Enormous thanks to **Glenys Livingstone** for allowing me to include an excerpt of one of my favorite books, *PaGaian Cosmology: Re-inventing Earth-based Goddess Religion*. You are so dear to my heart—and a tremendous inspiration to me.

Many thanks to **Rebekah Myers** for reviewing *Hallelujah Chorus*— and agreeing to sing Deborah's beautiful re-write at the last minute. I so appreciate your devotion to the Sisterhood and I love you dearly.

Appreciation to my beloved husband **Anders Løberg**, who designed the book cover and helped with website updates. Your love, support and many contributions made this book possible. You also managed to get me singing again, after a very long break. Thank you for bringing the music back to my heart love. I love you very much sweet.

My mom and I would also like to acknowledge her wonderful partner, **Rick Weiss**, for being an all-around awesome guy.

I would like to thank all who sang or played for us at the Solstice Sing-Alongs this year and last—**Shellee Layne** (2021), **Anders Løberg, Dale Allen, Kay and Dan Aldred, Megha Morganfield** and **Rebekah Myers.** Your voices and music brought these carols to life. Many thanks to my Circle Sisters—**Angelica Linnea** and **Leslie Ahern**— who joined us at our home.

I would also like to acknowledge my beloved Circle Sister, **Camilla Berge Wolff**, who usually sings with us. Although she could not make it to the Sing-Along, she popped by the Friday before and did an impromptu Facebook Live Sing-Along, which was a lot of fun!

Thank you to each contributor who took the time to carefully re-write these songs, shared wisdom, art or poetry. I love and appreciate all of you so much.

Many thanks to those who reviewed the book and wrote early endorsements—**Miriam Robbins Dexter, Liz Kelly, Byron Ballard**, and **Iris Eve**. We are honored by your words.

I would also like to offer my gratitude to **Sol Jonassen, Hildur Lilliendahl Viggósdóttir**, and **Miriam Robbins Dexter** for helping me get to the root origins of "Jul" in Norse.

I would like to thank my dear sisters **Tamara Albanna, Susan Morgaine, Jeanette Bjørnsen, Camilla Berge Wolff, Sharon Smith, Arlene Bailey, Tammy Nedrebø-Skurtveit, Arna Baartz, Kat Shaw, Kay Louise Aldred, Rebekah Myers,** and **Alyscia Cunningham** for always being right there to cheer me on in the spirit of true sisterhood.

I'd like to acknowledge my children, **Joey** and **Helani**, who have inspired all my work. I am tremendously proud of both of you—and I love you with all my heart.

Thank you to all our readers and Girl God supporters over the years. We love and appreciate you!

Sharon's Acknowledgments

I would like to acknowledge, first and foremost, my Dear Sister **Trista Hendren** for giving me the opportunity to be a part of Girl God Books. When I first discovered the Girl God FB page, I knew I was "home." And when Trista messaged me one day and asked if I would like to write something for her anthology, *On the Wings of Isis: Reclaiming the Sovereignty of Auset*, I was deeply touched and incredibly honored. Since then I have had several poems, articles and even a bit of my own original artwork in various other Girl God Books anthologies. Trista, you made my dream of becoming a published author a reality, and I can never thank you enough for that!

I want to thank **Pat Daly**, as well, for her dedication with helping to edit/proof this book and all of the Girl God Books publications. It is no easy job to be an Editor/Proofreader (I have done this professionally for many years, so I know)—her work here is deeply appreciated!

I would also like to thank my daughter, **Kelinda**, my greatest cheerleader, who believed in my ability to be a published writer, even when I didn't. I Love You, my Flame-haired Warrior Woman! Three hand squeezes!

Thanks also to my long-time sister-friend, **Dr. Bambi Lobdell, Ph.D.**, professor of English and Women's Studies at both the University of Binghamton and SUNY Oneonta in upstate New York, who created the course of study, "Witches, Whores, and Wild Women" and who authored the incredible book, *A Strange Sort of Being: The Transgender Life of Lucy Ann/Joseph Israel Lobdell, 1829-1912*, about one of her role-breaking ancestors. Bambi has been my inspiration since our days together at The Delaware River Writers Group, and she continues to inspire me to accomplish my goals as a writer, a story-teller, and a teacher.

Much gratitude to my mentor and dear sister-friend, **Colleen Russell, M.A.** Transpersonal Psychology, a student of Marion Woodman, an artist/writer (The Feminine Path to Wholeness: Becoming a Conscious Queen) and co-facilitator of women's retreats at beautiful Scotia House in the Pacific Northwest. Colleen guided me on my Healing Journey as a woman seeking to reconnect with her authentic self and voice. Colleen's wisdom and gentle teachings changed my life!

Thanks, as well, to my dear sister (and the Scotia House Fairy), **Sandee Meade**, whose constant support and encouragement enabled me to begin to believe in myself. Thanks for allowing me to live at Scotia House and heal there for two years: It was MAGICAL!

And finally, thanks and so much love to the following young women whom I've heart-adopted over the years, who have blessed my life in so many ways: **Angie Metzner, Michele Chaney, Karen Pogorzelski,** and **Renee Jamerson**. You are each amazing young women — Overcomers and Wise, Wild Women in your own right. I am so immensely proud of you all and so honored to consider you "heart-daughters"!

If you enjoyed this book, please consider writing a brief review on Amazon and/or Goodreads.

We LOVE photos of our readers with Girl God Books! Please post on social media to spread the word – or email them to support@girlgod.org.

What's Next?!

Rainbow Goddess – Celebrating Neurodiversity – Edited by Kay Louise Aldred, Tamara Albanna, Trista Hendren and Pat Daly

Women's Sovereignty and Body Autonomy Beyond Roe v. Wade – Edited by Arlene Bailey, Pat Daly, Sharon Smith and Trista Hendren

Kali Rising: Sacred Rage – Edited by C. Ara Campbell, Jaclyn Cherie, Pat Daly, and Trista Hendren

Pain Perspectives: Finding Meaning in the Fire – Edited by Kay Louise Aldred, Trista Hendren and Pat Daly

Making Love with the Divine: Sacred, Ecstatic, Erotic Experiences – Kay Louise Aldred

Embodied Structure: Creating Safe Space for Learning, Facilitating and Sharing – Kay Louise Aldred and Dan Aldred

Goddess Chants and Songs Book – Edited by Trista Hendren, Anique Radiant Heart and Pat Daly

Out of Darkness She Speaks: A Rich Anthology of Poetry and Artwork Inspired by the Feminine – Leonor Murciano-Luna, Ph.D.

Lotus Heart: The Compassion of Kuan Yin – Edited by Trista Hendren, Herng Yu Tzong, and Yeshe Matthews

And Still, I Rise – Kat Shaw

Other: Anthologies and children's books on the Black Madonna, Mary Magdalene, Mother Mary, Aradia, Kali, Brigid, Sophia, Spider Woman, Persephone and Hecate are also in the works.

http://thegirlgod.com/publishing.php

CPSIA information can be obtained
at www.ICGtesting.com
Printed in the USA
LVHW030540201222
735537LV00007B/821